The Chess Ladder

The Chess Ladder, 2023 - 88 pages
By Olivier Pire

Copyright © The Chess Ladder, 2023

Production, Content, Design, Illustration, Edition, by Olivier Pire
With the support of Nombril (nombril.be) for the covers design

ISBN 978-2-8052-0933-8

The Chess Ladder

A Step-by-step Guide for Kids to Learn Chess

Olivier Pire

Table of Contents

Hello futur Chess Player !

Welcome to The Chess Ladder and to the big and exciting family of Chess enthusiasts.

My name is Olivier Pire, I am a Chess player with great passion for the game. I am also a Certified Chess School Instructor for the International Federation of Chess (FIDE). For many years, I have been teaching Chess in International Schools, Sports Centers, Private Schools and online, to numerous young enthusiasts from age 4 to age 12 from around the World.

This handbook is a compilation of my teaching method for Beginners, refined and improved over time, aiming to ensure that children grasp joy playing the game but also enhance their understanding of it, reveal their character and ultimately, but very important, to help them discover their own cognitions, and enjoy playing with it for the long term.

I was 10 years old, repeatedly asking my parents and sister to play with me. Exceptionaly my loving mother would. This desire I had to push the pieces on the board and set a trap for her King was unfortunately rare. This book is a message of love to this boy I once was, and it is my gift to all young boys and girls willing to learn the wonderful game of Chess.

Who's this Book for ?

I embarked on writing this book with the aim of reaching children who may not have had the opportunity to experience chess in their lives. It's somewhat akin to not having a bicycle around to spark curiosity and ultimately enjoy a ride. Just as lacking a nearby lake, sea, or river denies the chance to be curious about and learn to swim or sail. If chess has

never been part of your world, you're missing out on a significant opportunity to enhance your life. This book is thoughtfully designed for anyone eager to learn chess from the very beginning, progressing at a comfortable pace. It's suitable for children aged 4 and above, as well as for parents, schoolteachers, and educators at

educational or recreational centers who wish to introduce children (and themselves in the process) to the world of chess.

How to use this Book ?

Within these pages, you'll find all the fundamental concepts, including Attack, Check, Defense, and more, presented in an intuitive and logical manner: Theory, Practice, and a multitude of puzzles. Along the way, we'll touch on other topics like 'playing with a clock' 'playing online,' and the 'Benefits of Chess,' offering insights to young players and pedagogical ideas to parents, teachers, and coaches. Each chapter concludes with an Award that I encourage you to aim for. Finally, at the end of the book, a test wraps up the chess ladder apprenticeship.

P.S. Just as chess problems are meant to be solved, illustrations along the book are meant for kids to color!

A very short history of Chess

Earliest Texts referring to the origins of Chess date from the beginning of the 7th century, but earlier evidence of Chess is found in nearby Sasanian Persia around 600 A.D. - Chatrang was taken up

by the Muslim world after the Islamic conquest of Persia (633–51). One of theses texts explains that Chatrang, "Chess" in Pahlavi, was introduced to Persia by 'Dewasarm, a great ruler of India' during the reign of Khosrow I.
The early forms of Chess in India were known as chaturanga, literally "four divisions" of the infantry, cavalry, elephants, and chariotry – represented by pieces that would later evolve into the modern pawn, knight, bishop, and rook, respectively. Thence it spread eastward and westward along the Silk Road where the game came to be known by the name Chatrang.
The oldest archaeological chess artifacts – ivory pieces – were excavated in today's Samarkand, in Uzbekistan, Central Asia, and date to about 760, with some of them possibly being older. Remarkably, almost all findings of the oldest pieces come from along the Silk Road. Xiangqi is the form of Chess best known in China, and refer to a game from 569 A.D. at the latest, but it has not been proven if this game was or was not

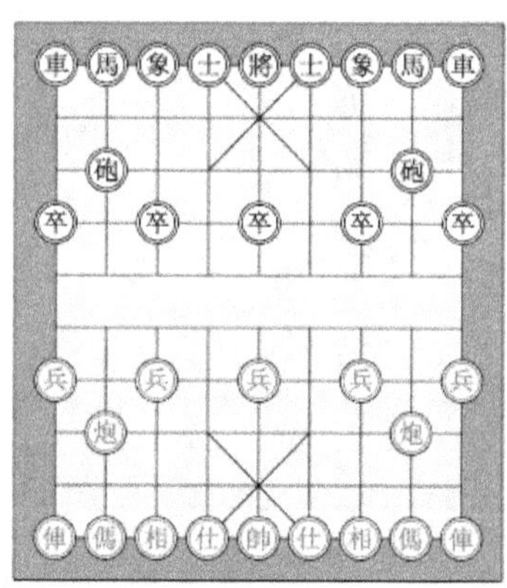

Xiangqi

directly related to chess. The eastern migration of Chess, into China and Southeast Asia, has even less documentation than its migration west, making it largely conjectured.

Around 1200, the rules of shatranj started to be modified in Spain before diffusing into the rest of Europe. In the 18th century, the center of European chess life moved from Southern Europe to mainland France where Romanticism brought new ways of playing the game.

As the 19th century progressed, chess organization developed quickly. Many chess clubs, chess books, and chess journals appeared. There were correspondence matches between cities and Chess problems became a regular part of newspapers. In 1851, was held in London the first modern Chess Tournament.

Wilhelm Steinitz, the first official World Chess Champion, from 1886 to 1894

Vera Menchik, the first Women's World Chess Champion, in 1927

In 1924, in Paris, was created FIDE, the International Chess Federation,

which is today one of the largest sport governing bodies, encompassing 199 countries as affiliate members, in the form of National Chess Federations.

Chess is nowadays a truly global sport, with dozens of millions of players in all the continents, and more than 60 million games on average played every day.

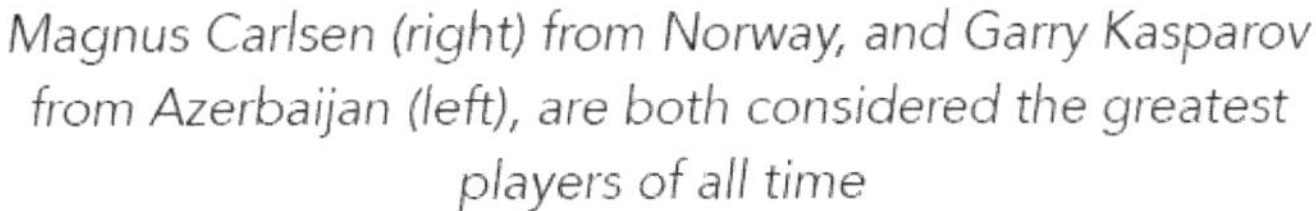

Magnus Carlsen (right) from Norway, and Garry Kasparov from Azerbaijan (left), are both considered the greatest players of all time

The Chess Board

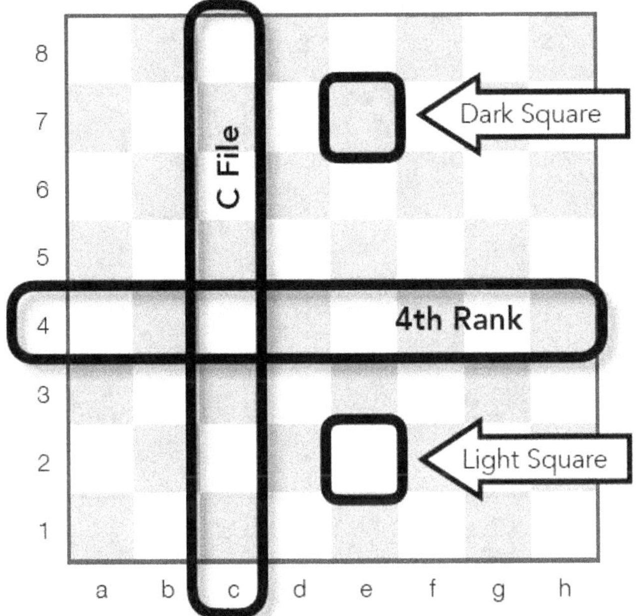

Dark and Light colours are used to distinguish squares. Numbers and Letters are used to name each square.

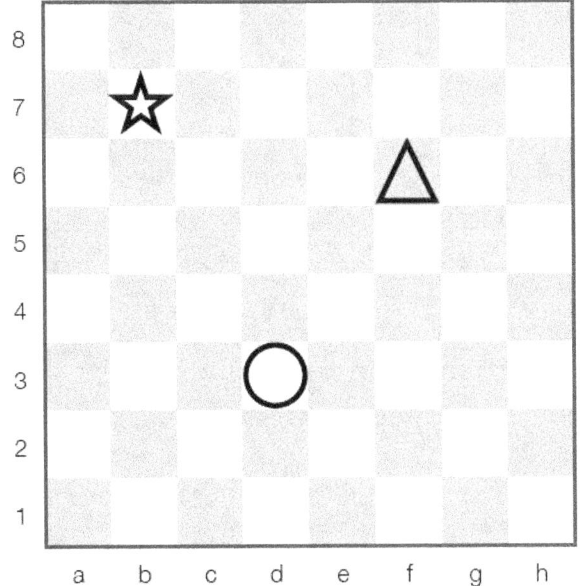

On which square is the Star ?
On which square is the Triangle ?
On which square is the Circle ?

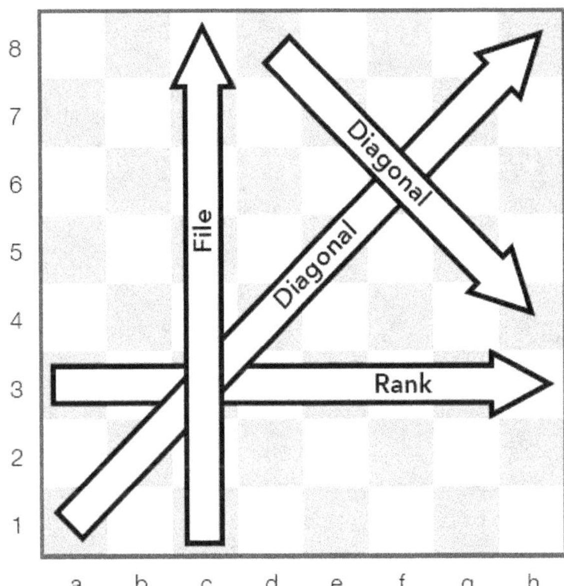

Rank, File and Diagonal are the words used to indicate how a piece moves.

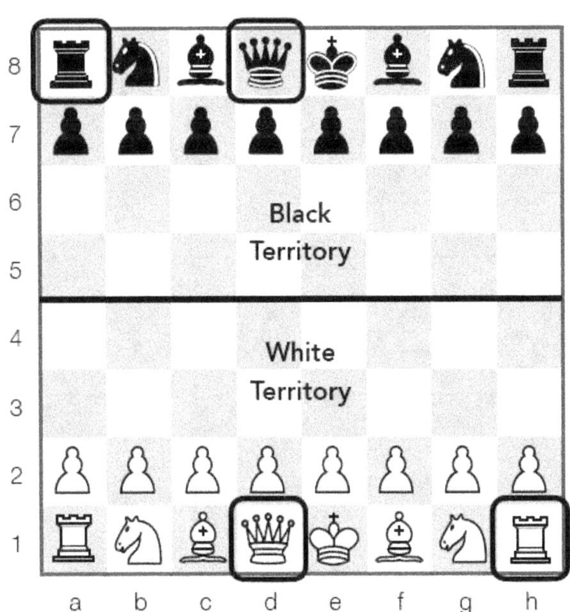

When you start a game:

- white pieces are on ranks 1 & 2
- If the board has no coordinates, make sure to have a white square at each player's right hand corner.
- Have the white Queen on a light square and the black Queen on a dark square.

The Right Square

Practice

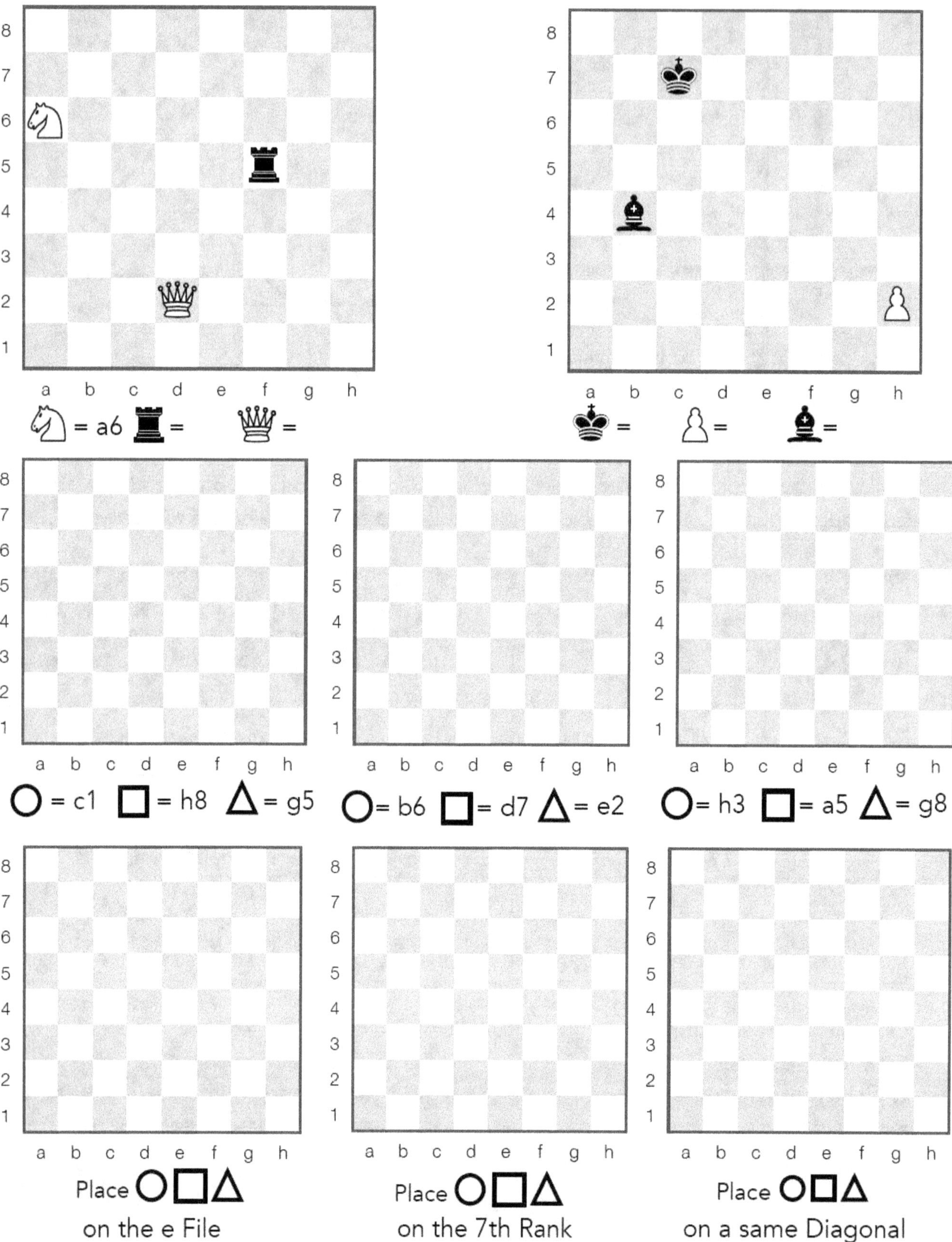

Place ◯ ▢ △
on the e File

Place ◯ ▢ △
on the 7th Rank

Place ◯ ▢ △
on a same Diagonal

Chicken on the Board !   Practice

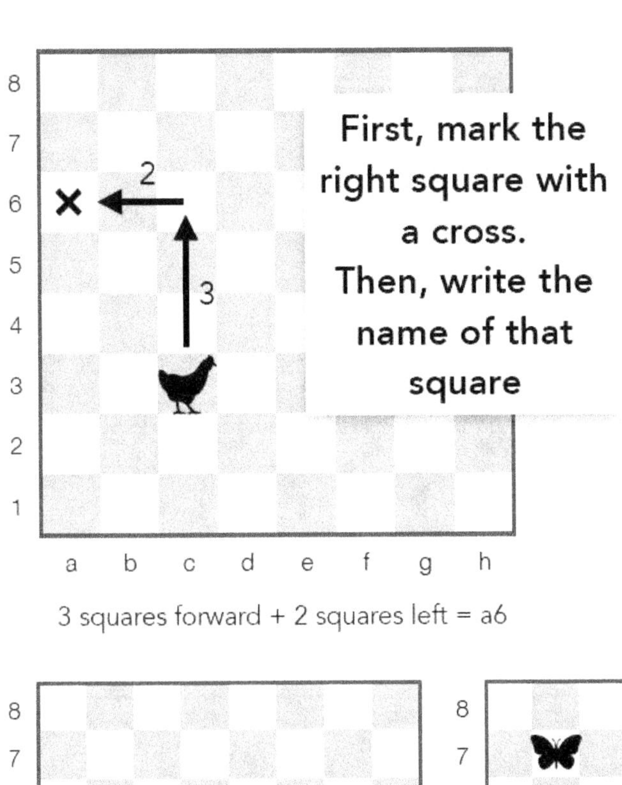

3 squares forward + 2 squares left = a6

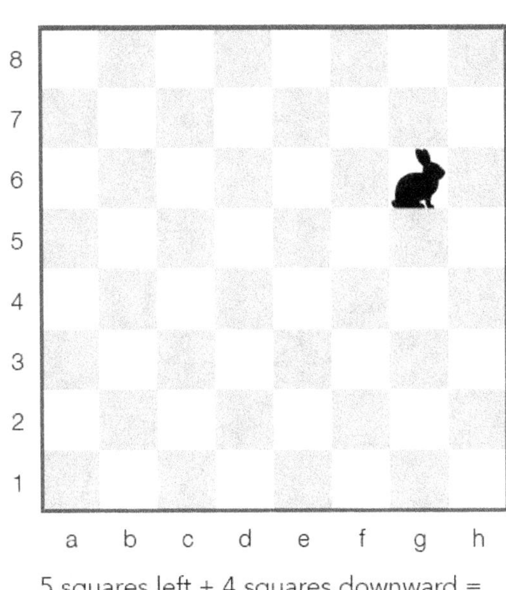

5 squares left + 4 squares downward =

2 squares right
+ 3 squares forward =

1 square left
+ 6 squares downward =

5 squares downward
+ 3 squares right =

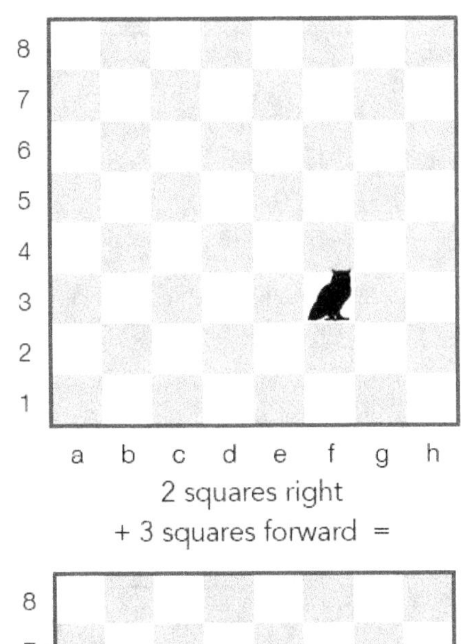

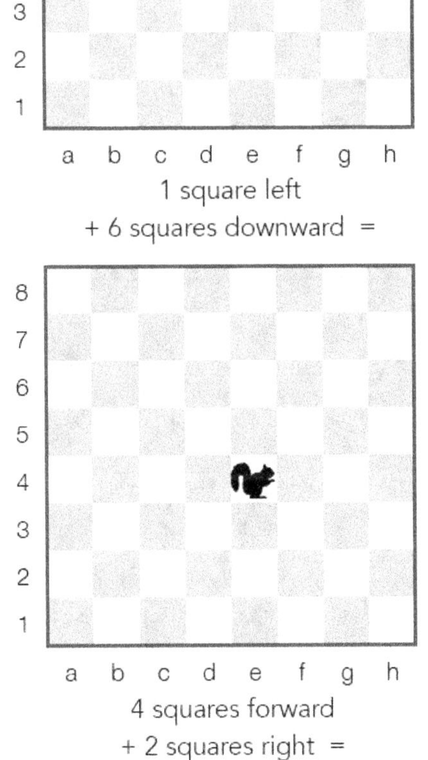

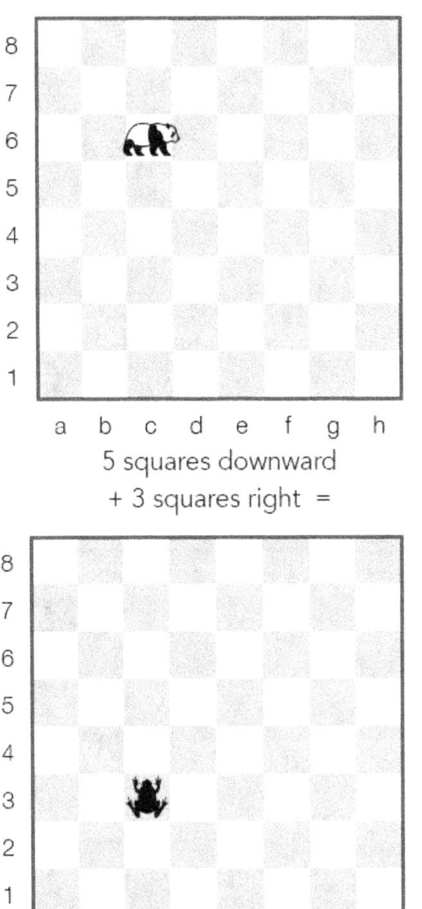

1 square downward
+ 3 squares right =

4 squares forward
+ 2 squares right =

2 squares left
+ 5 squares forward =

Chicken on the Board 2   Practice

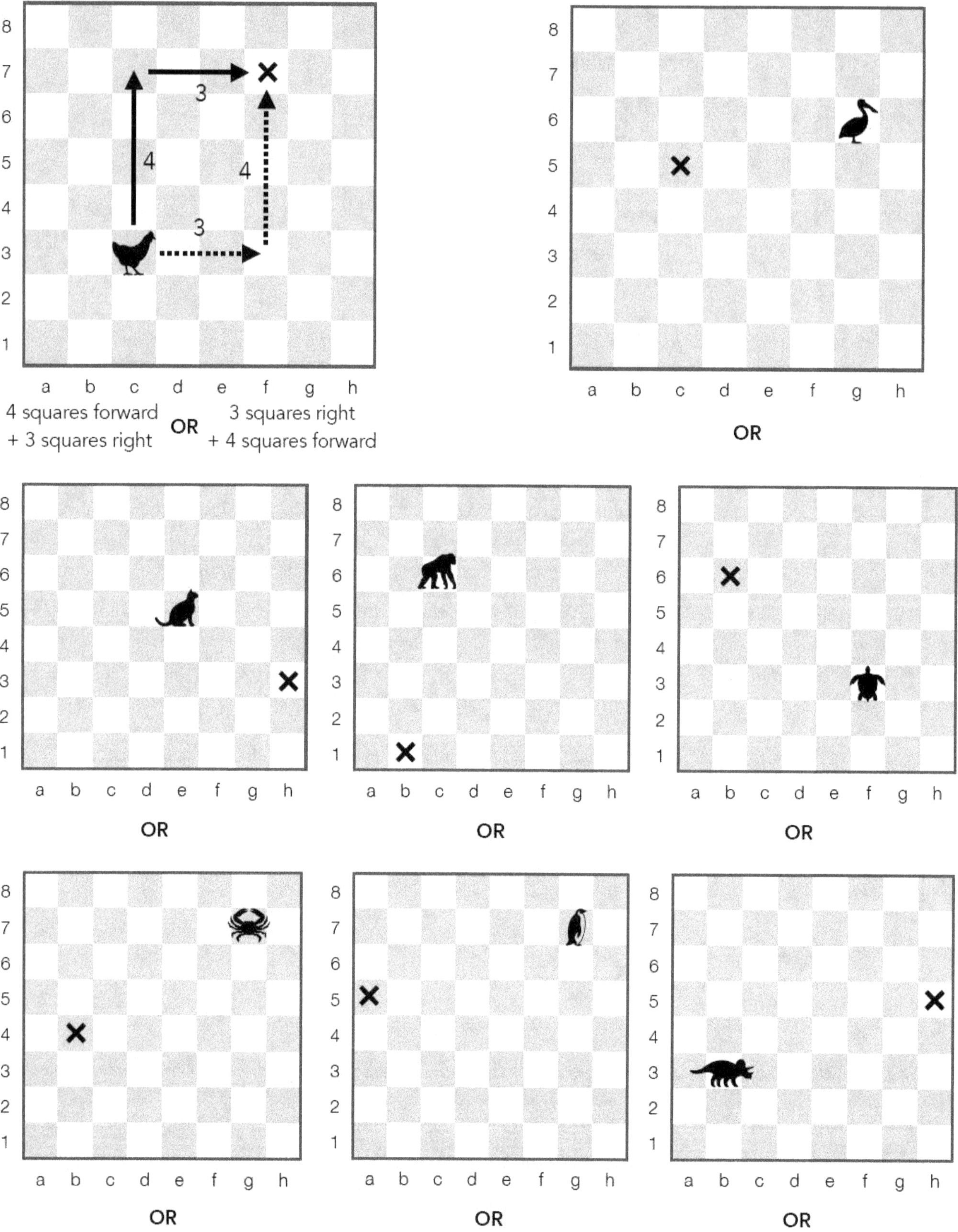

Board Orientation   Practice

As you may already know, the chessboard consists of squares with only two colors. For instance, if the c2 square is light-colored, you can conclude that squares directly below it (c1) and above it (c3) are dark-colored. Similarly, you can deduce that squares to the left of it (b2) and to the right of it (d2) are also dark-colored. To practice this spatial logic, take a moment to observe the board below, and then <u>visualize it mentally</u> for the upcoming questions. Ask a partner to grab a board and correct you right away.

<u>What is the colour?</u>
- If b6 is dark, what colour is c5?
- If e2 is light, what colour is e6?
- If f7 is light, what colour is g8?
- If a1 is dark, what colour is d4?
- What colour is d8?

<u>On which square am I?</u>
- From d7, I move 1 square to the right, and then 2 squares down. On which square am I?
- From a4, I go 3 squares up, and 4 squares to the right. On which square am I?
- From g5 square, I move down 2 squares, and then I go 4 squares left. Which square am I?

<u>Guide me to the right square</u>
- I am on c2. Guide me to b5: c3 up, c4 up, c5 up, b5 left !
- I am on h6, guide me to g7
- I am on e4, guide me to f1
- I am on b3, guide me to a6
- I am on d7, guide me to c4

I CAN READ THE BOARD

Board
Award

The Chess Pieces

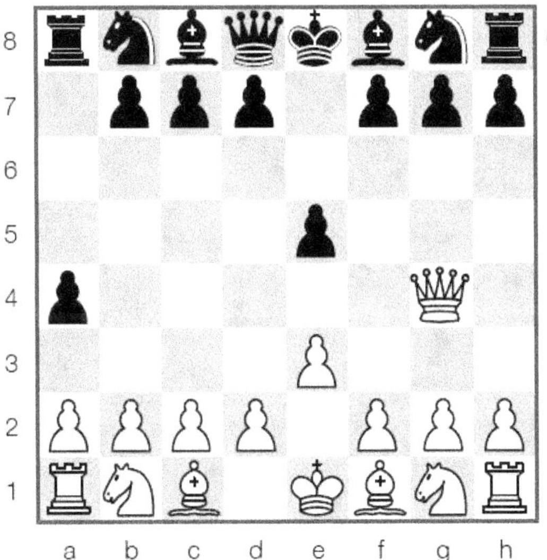

In this book, Chess Puzzles look like this:

This black dot means it is black pieces turn to play

Annotations

d2d4 indicates the pawn on d2 moves to d4

Nf3 indicates a Knight moves to f3

Bc4 indicates a Bishop moves to c4

Ra5 indicates a Rook moves to a5

Qf6 indicates the Queen moves to f6

Kd1 indicates the King moves to d1

If there is a piece beside the board, you should use it to solve the puzzle

The Rook

- Each player starts with 2 Rooks.
- The Rook moves in straight lines, either vertically (forward, backward) or horizontally (sideways), covering one or multiple squares at a time.
- Rooks cannot jump over other pieces.
- The Rook is valued at 5 pawns

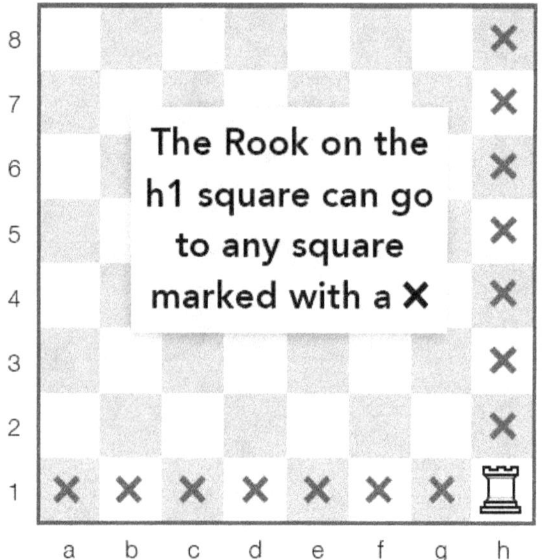

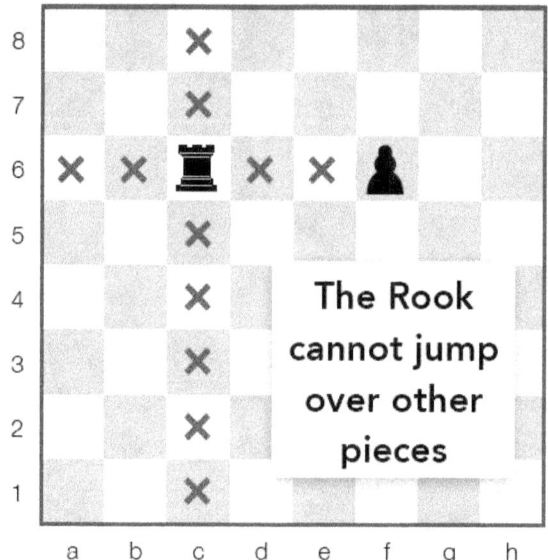

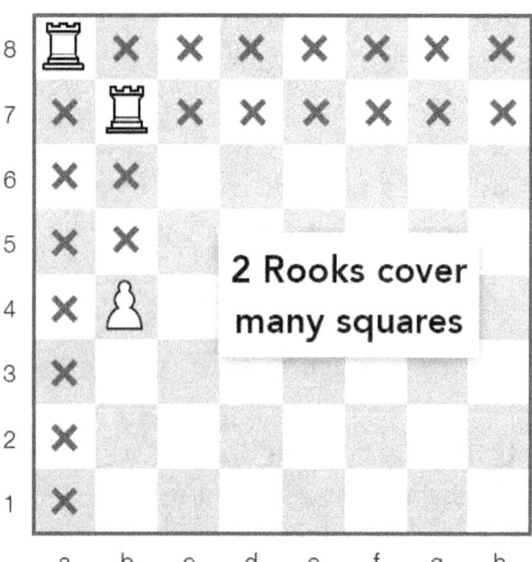

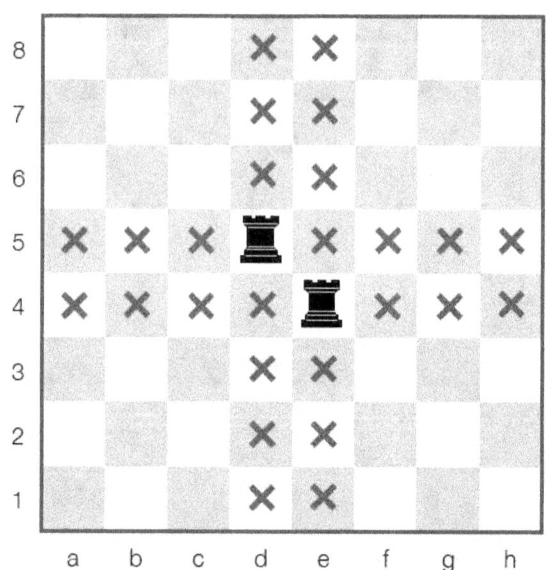

The Bishop

- Each player begins a game with 2 Bishops.
- The Bishop moves diagonally on the board, covering one or multiple squares at a time.
- Bishops cannot jump over other pieces.
- The Bishop is typically considered as having a value of 3 pawns

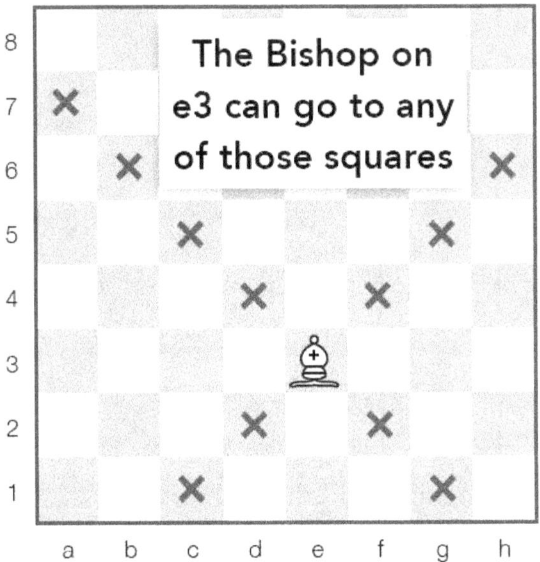

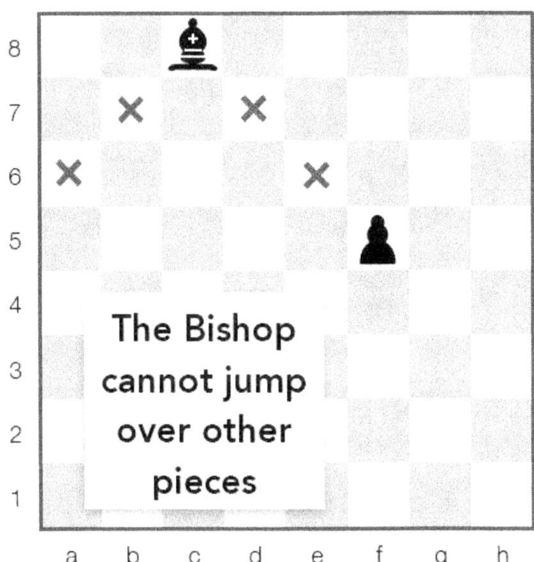

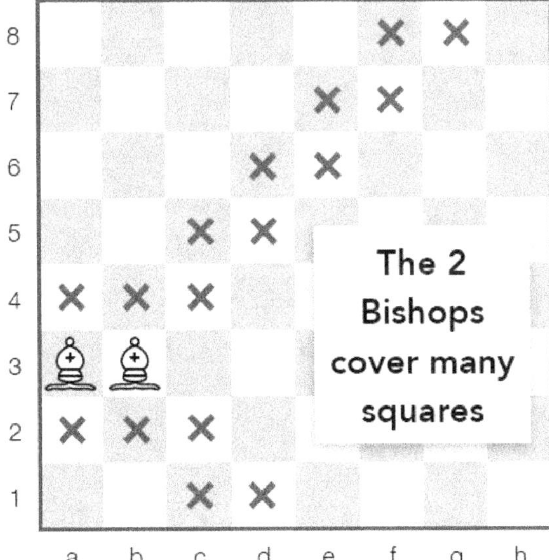

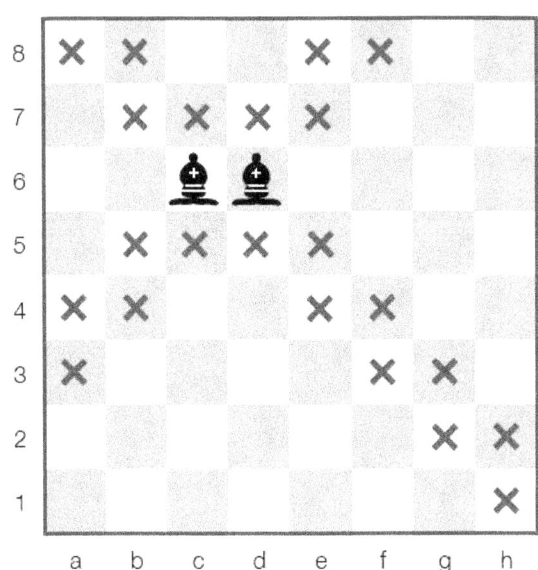

The Queen

- In Chess, each player starts with 1 Queen.
- The Queen is the most versatile piece on the board. It can move diagonally, horizontally, or vertically, covering one or multiple squares at a time.
- Queens cannot jump over other pieces.
- The Queen is the strongest piece on the board. She has the value of 9 pawns

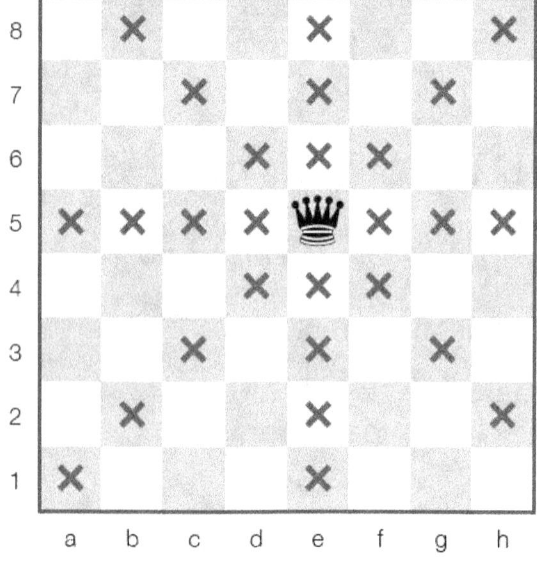

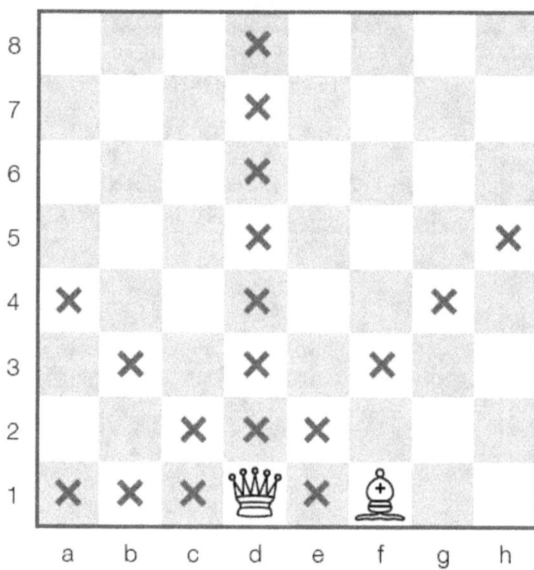

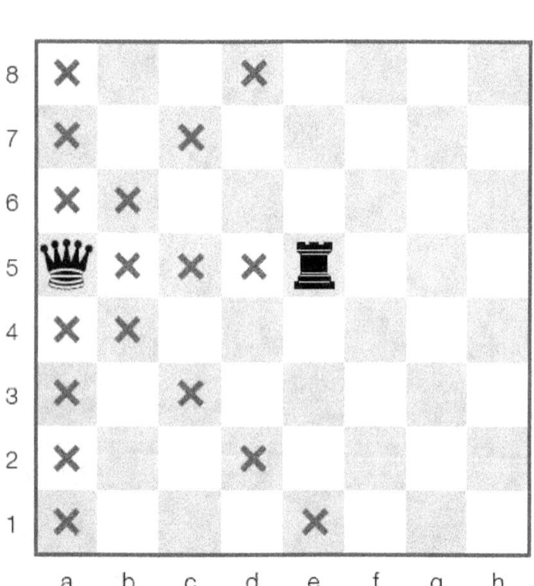

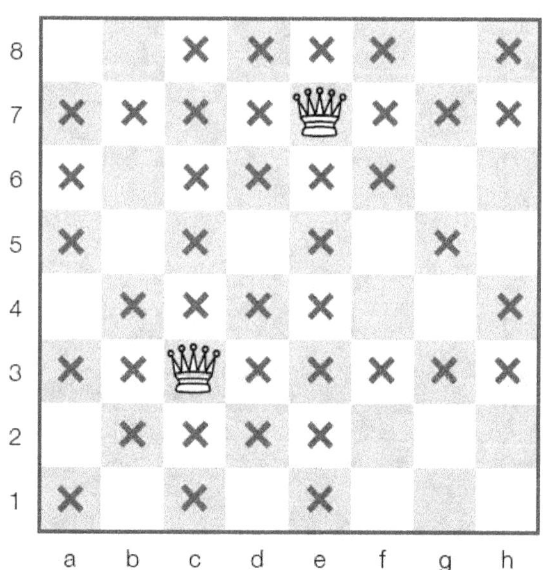

Pieces Reach   Practice

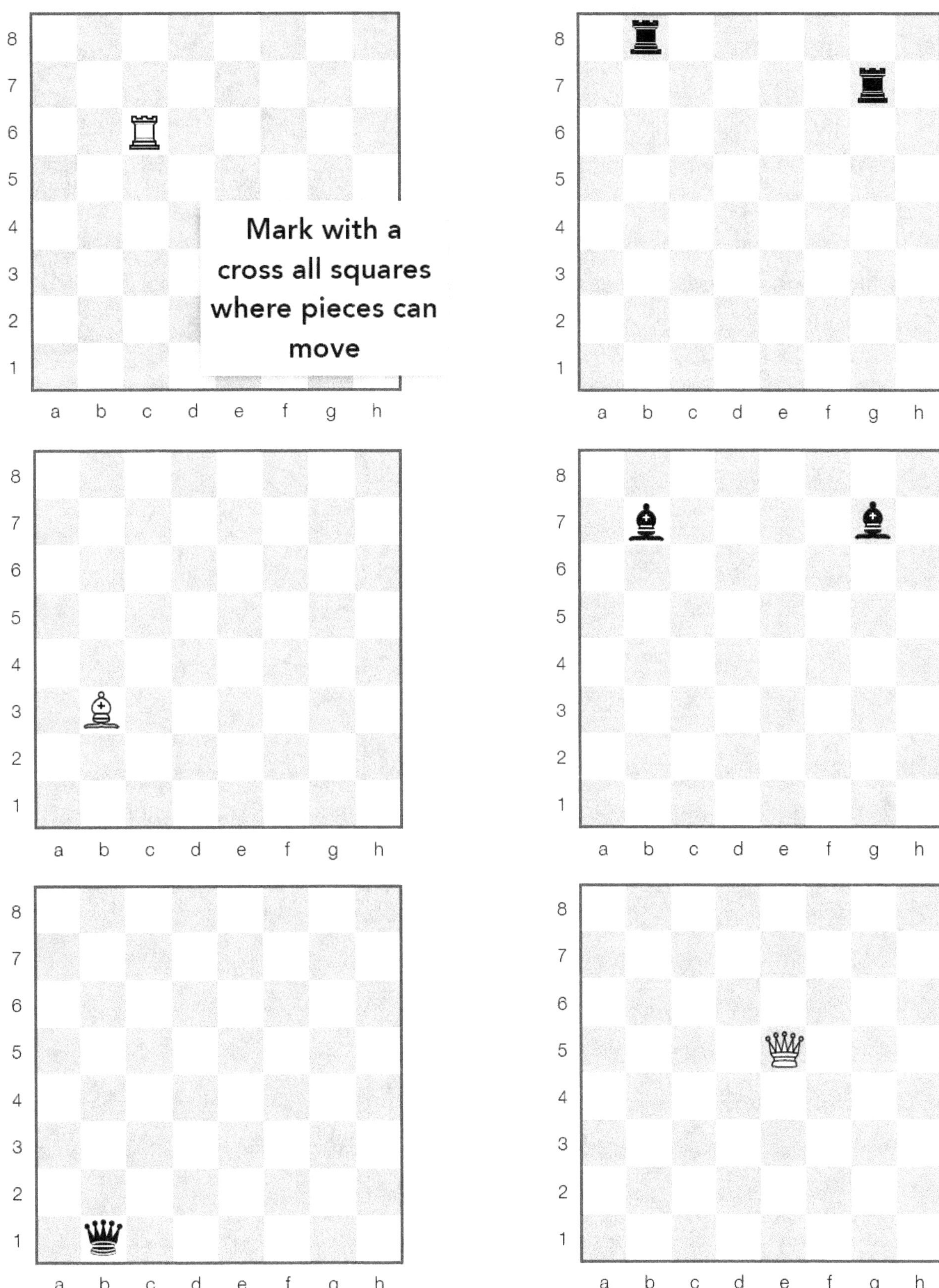

The King

- Each player has 1 King
- The King moves like the Queen but only one square at a time.
- The King cannot jump over other pieces.
- The King is the most important piece of the game of Chess.
- The two Kings can never stand side by side.
- Unlike other pieces, the King cannot move to a square that is under attack or threatened by the opponent's pieces.

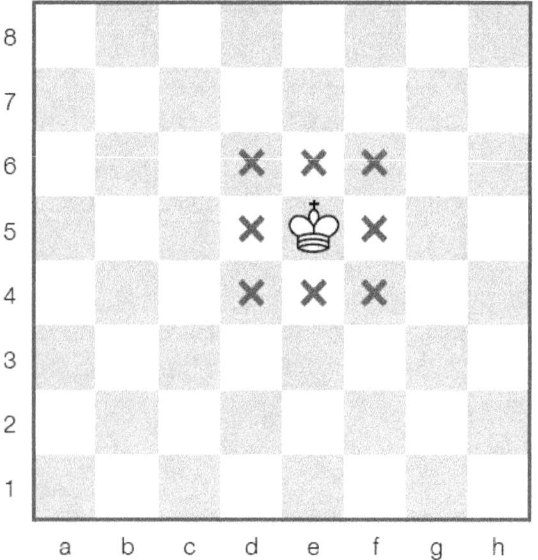

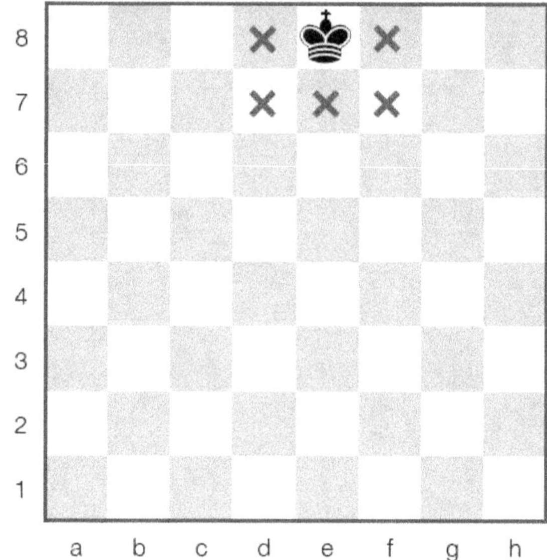

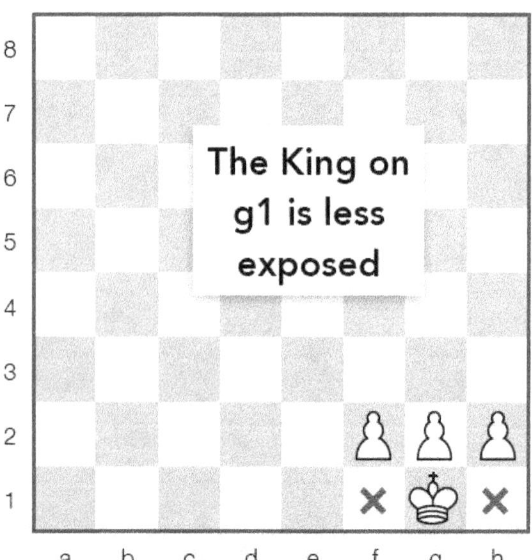

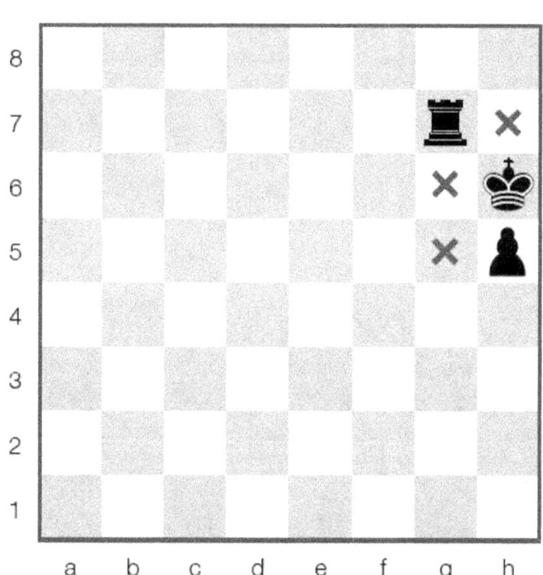

The Knight

- Each player starts with 2 Knights
- It moves in an "L" shape: two squares in one direction (either horizontally or vertically) and then one square at a right angle to that movement.
- The Knight is the only piece that can jump over other pieces
- A Knight on a light square will move to a dark square, and vice versa.
- Each Knight is valued at 3 pawns.

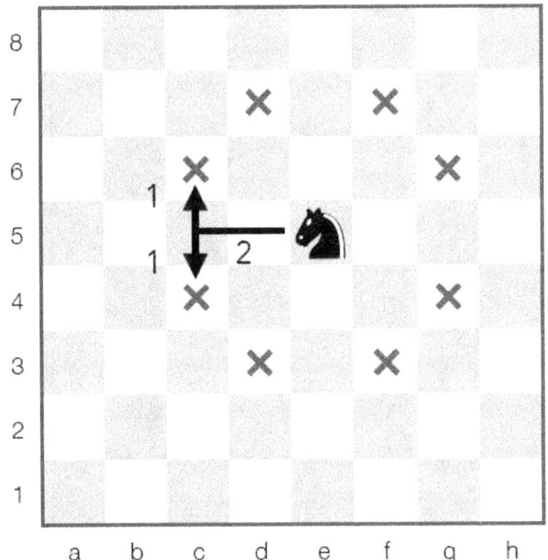

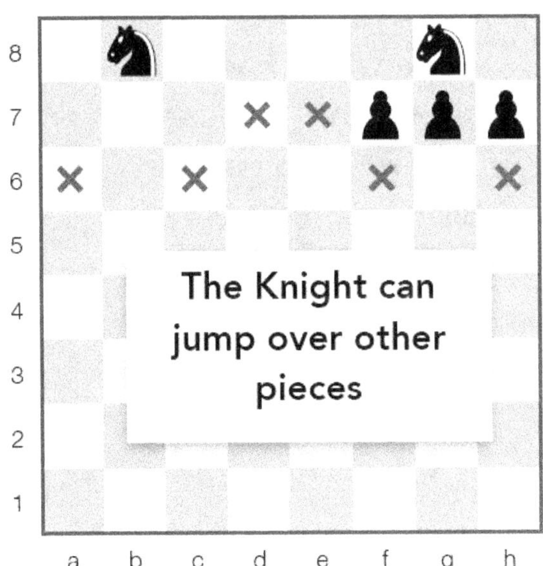

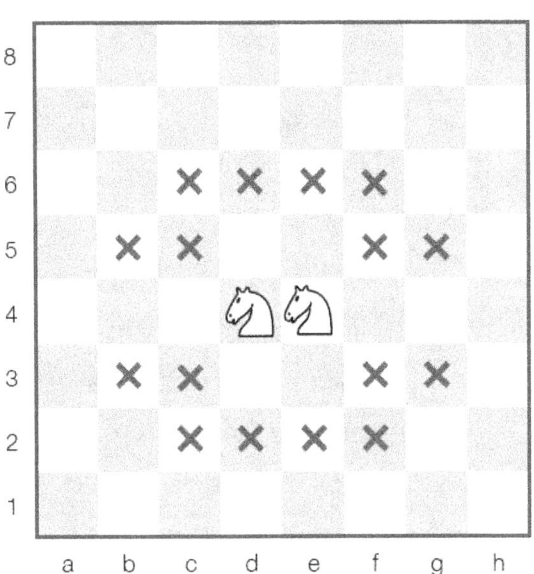

The Pawn

- In Chess, each player starts with 8 Pawns, forming the front line of their army.
- On their initial move, Pawns have the option to move forward two squares.
- The Pawn is the only piece that moves differently than it captures. It moves 1 square forward at a time only, and captures diagonally only.
- The Pawn cannot jump over other pieces nor move backward or sideways.
- The Pawn can promote into another piece by reaching the last opposite rank (explained in detail a bit further)

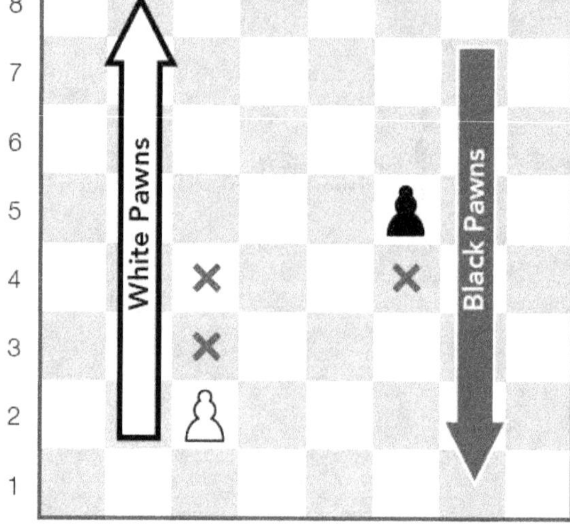

 On a 2D board, black pawns go down, and white pawns go up

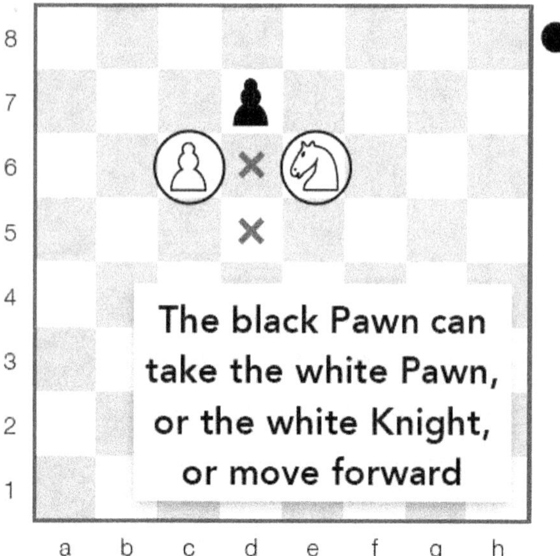

The black Pawn can take the white Pawn, or the white Knight, or move forward

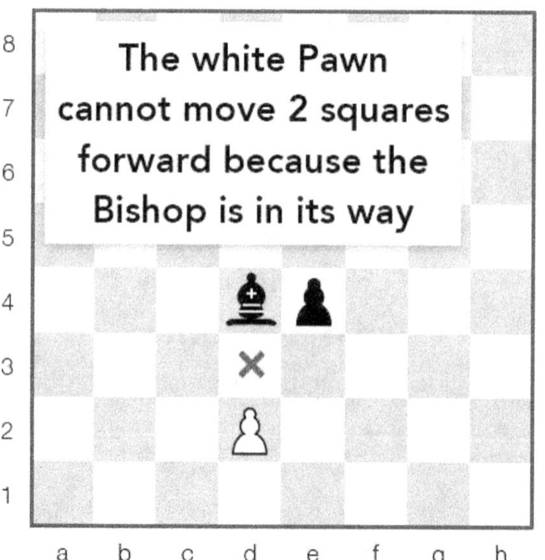

The white Pawn cannot move 2 squares forward because the Bishop is in its way

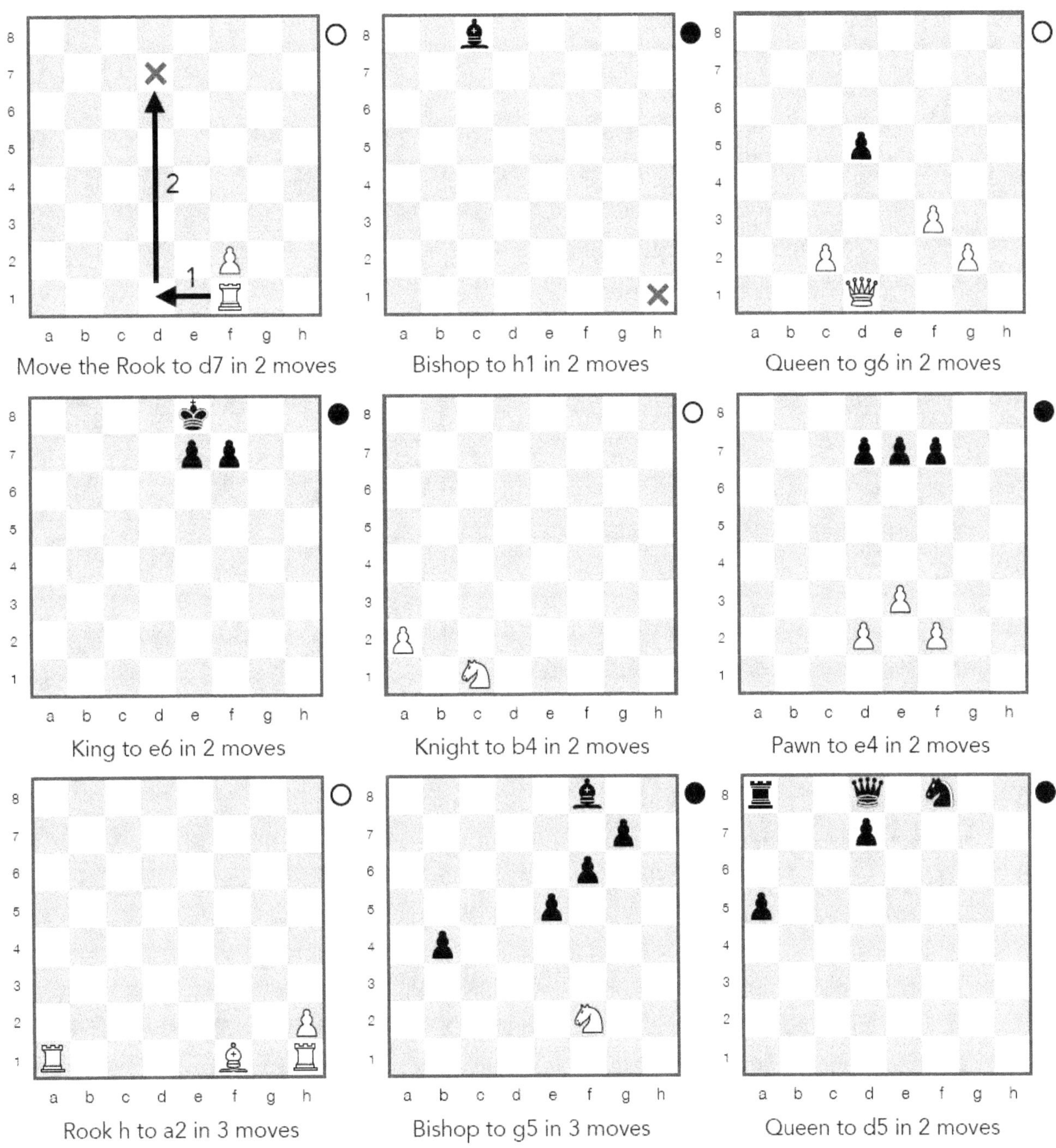

Move the Rook to d7 in 2 moves
Bishop to h1 in 2 moves
Queen to g6 in 2 moves
King to e6 in 2 moves
Knight to b4 in 2 moves
Pawn to e4 in 2 moves
Rook h to a2 in 3 moves
Bishop to g5 in 3 moves
Queen to d5 in 2 moves

Pieces Reach 2 Practice

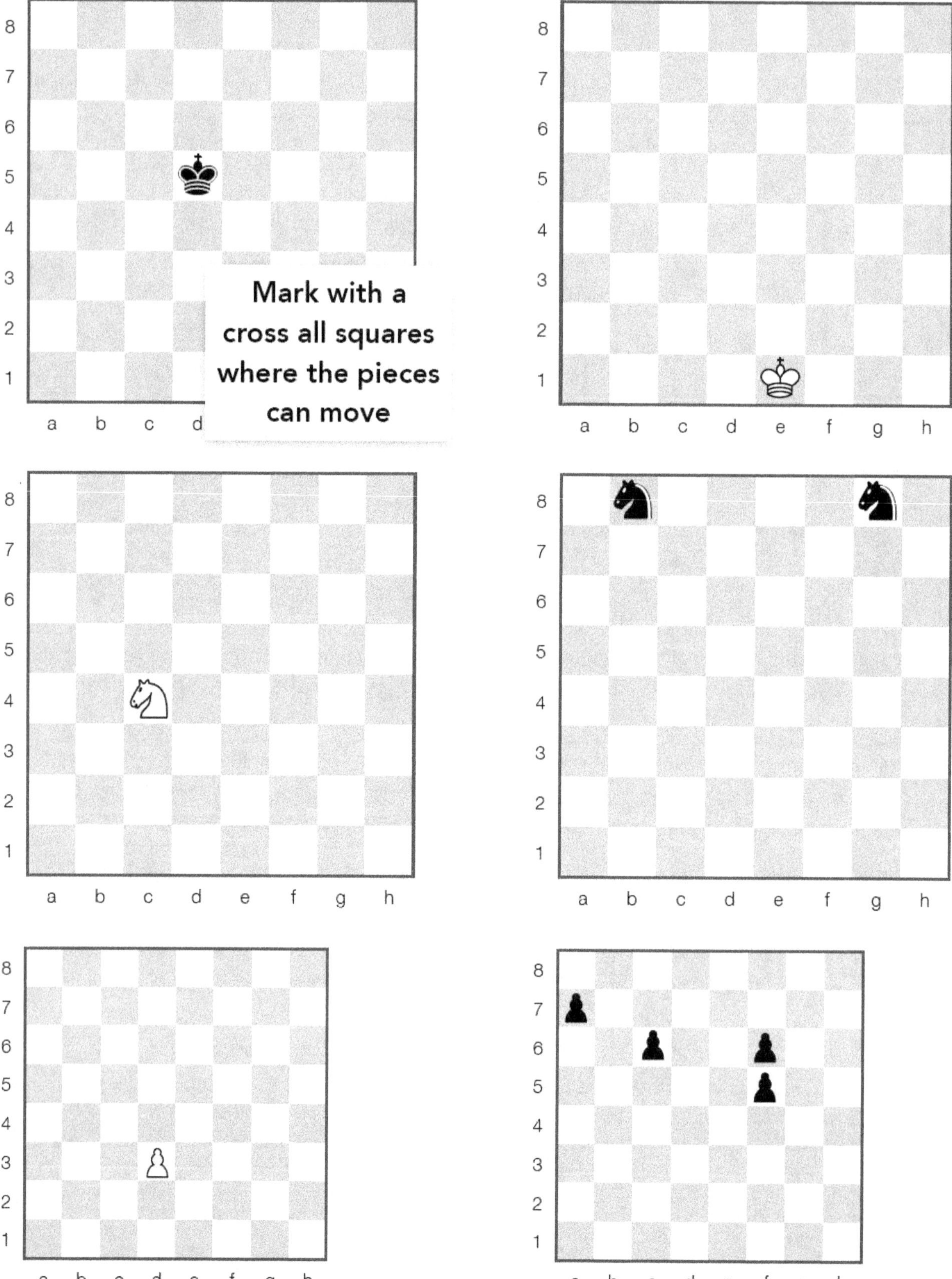

Goal of the Game

Now that you have a grasp of the chessboard, the pieces, and their movement, let's delve deeper into the objectives of the game of Chess. To secure victory in Chess, your ultimate goal is to confine your opponent's King. It's important to note that we don't say "take" or "capture" the King because direct capture of the King is not allowed in Chess.

So, how do you go about trapping the opponent's King? The strategy involves maneuvering your pieces strategically to encircle the King, essentially forcing it into a position where it has no legal moves left. This situation is known as "Checkmate," and it signifies your victory in the game.

Now, let's discuss how to shield your own King from getting trapped. The King is a relatively slow-moving piece compared to others on the board, making it vulnerable to attack. To safeguard your King, you need to utilize your other pieces to create a defensive perimeter around it. If you find yourself short on protective pieces, you have the option to promote your pawns into more powerful pieces. Additionally, early in the game, you can execute a maneuver called "castling." This involves moving your King to a corner of the board, typically behind a line of pawns, and positioning a Rook alongside it for added protection.

Best of luck in your
Chess endeavors!

I CAN MOVE THE PIECES

Moving
Pieces
Award

Games of Move & Take

Engaging in practice sessions with a classmate, coach, or parents using the following setups will enhance the student's understanding of the possibilities inherent in the mobility of each chess piece. These games should be played allowing ample time for the student to consider their next move. It's advisable for both players to take turns using black and white pieces, and it's recommended that they play a minimum of five games for each setup.

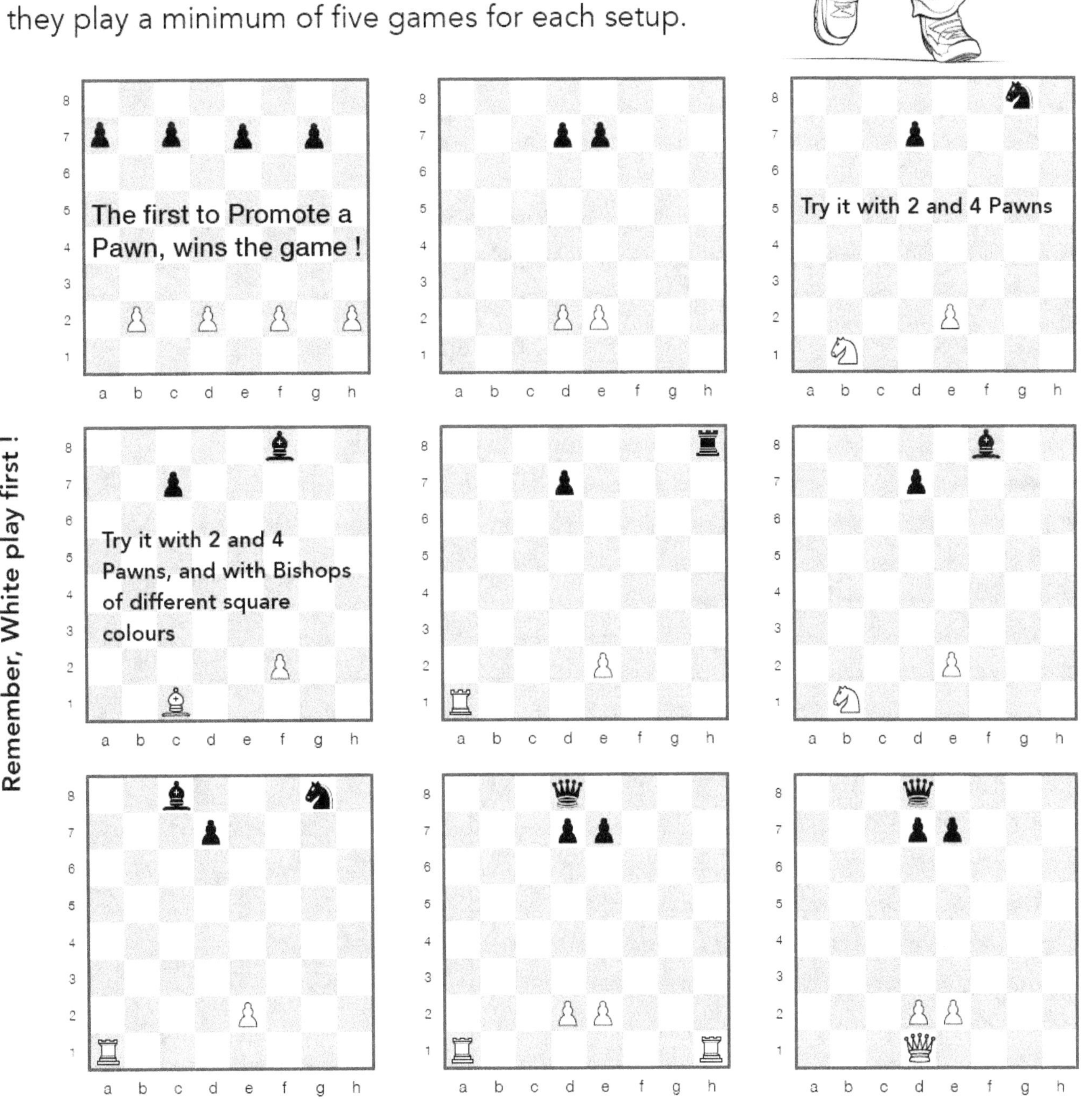

Promotion

In Chess, Promotion is the replacement of a Pawn with a new piece when the Pawn is moved to its last rank.
The player replaces the Pawn immediately with a Queen, Rook, Bishop, or Knight of the same color.
The new piece does not have to be a previously captured piece.
Promotion is mandatory; the Pawn cannot remain as a Pawn.

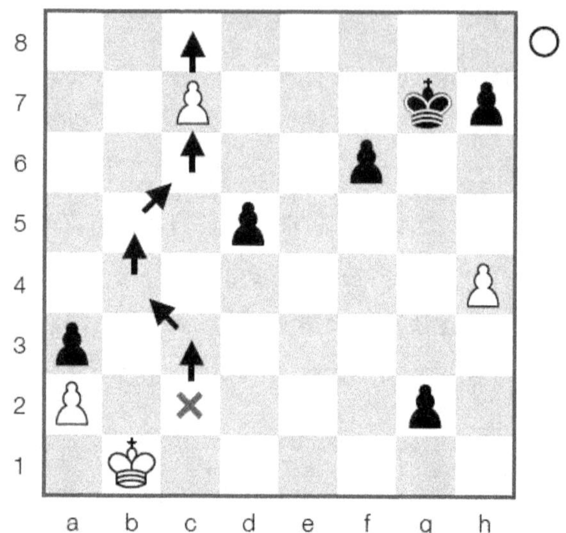

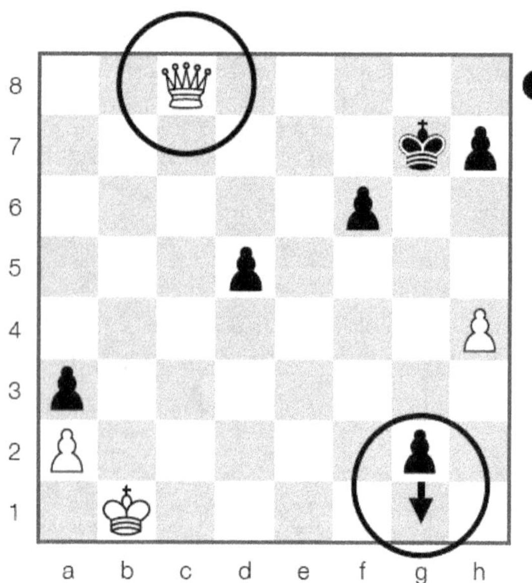

Promotion to a Queen is commonly referred to as 'queening,' while promotion to any other piece is known as 'underpromotion.'

Promotion is almost always to a Queen because it is the most powerful piece. Why choose another piece, after all?

As a result, a player might end up with two or more Queens or three or more Rooks, Bishops, or Knights.

In theory, a player could have as many as nine Queens, ten Knights, ten Bishops, or ten Rooks, although these scenarios are highly improbable.

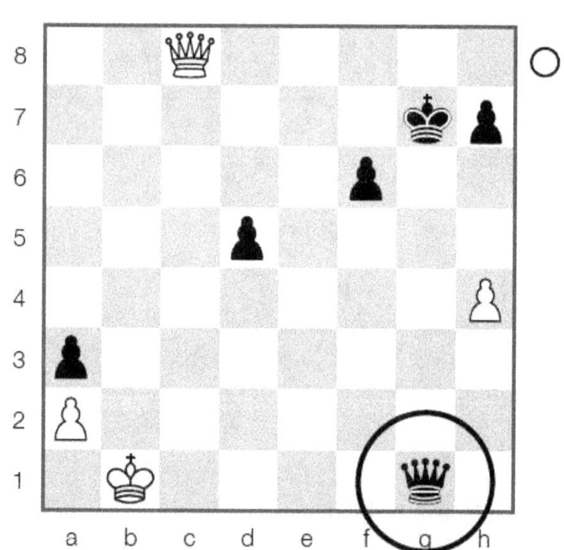

Move & Take Pieces Puzzles

The tactile experience of maneuvering chess pieces on a real Chess board can be particularly delightful, especially when a student discovers he/she can successfully capture an opponent's piece. Through this interactive experience, students naturally come to understand that a Queen possesses higher value than a Bishop because it covers a larger number of squares in a single move.

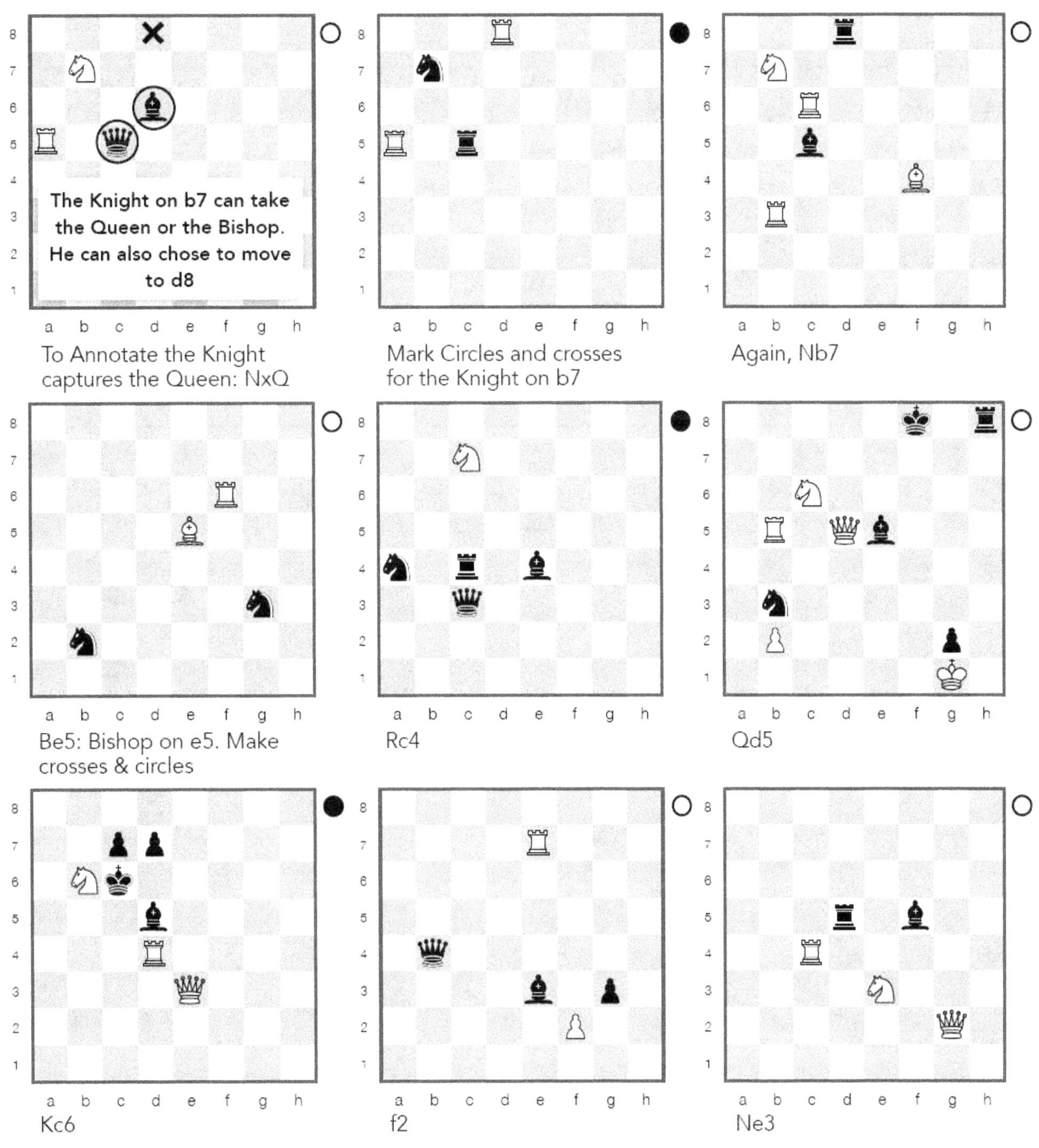

To Annotate the Knight
captures the Queen: NxQ

Mark Circles and crosses
for the Knight on b7

Again, Nb7

Be5: Bishop on e5. Make
crosses & circles

Rc4

Qd5

Kc6

f2

Ne3

Move & Take Pieces 2

Let's do more Circles & Crosses !

Puzzles

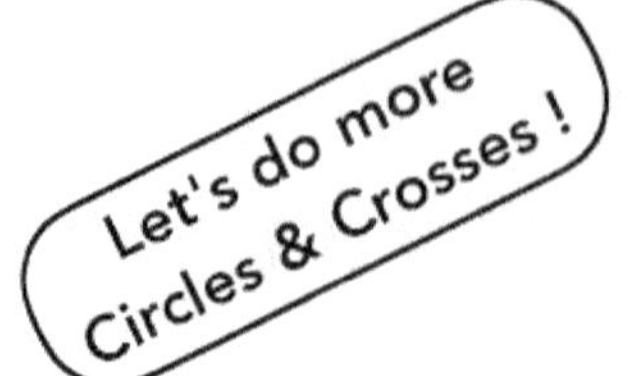

In these Puzzles, the student will face new situations with squares the piece can move to being under attack, and pieces to take being protected. The student may not see them yet, but we will welcome his/her comments about it, such as: "should I take it if they will take me back ?", "should I move to this square if they can take me ?". If it is the case, we will let the student include it when solving these puzzles. On the opposite, If the student does not see these threats yet, we will stick to the essential goal of piece movement and piece capture without other concerns.

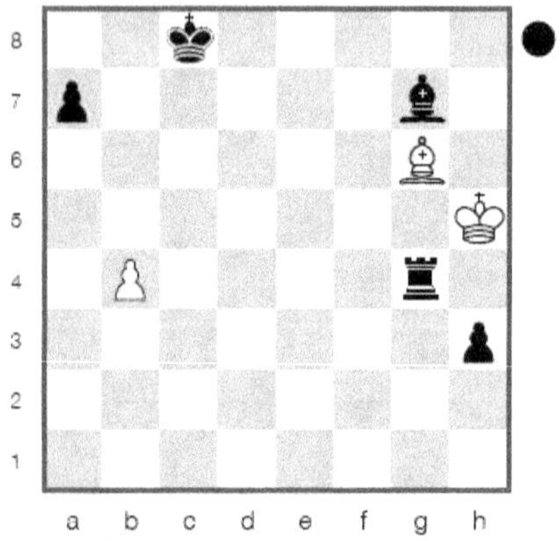

Rg4

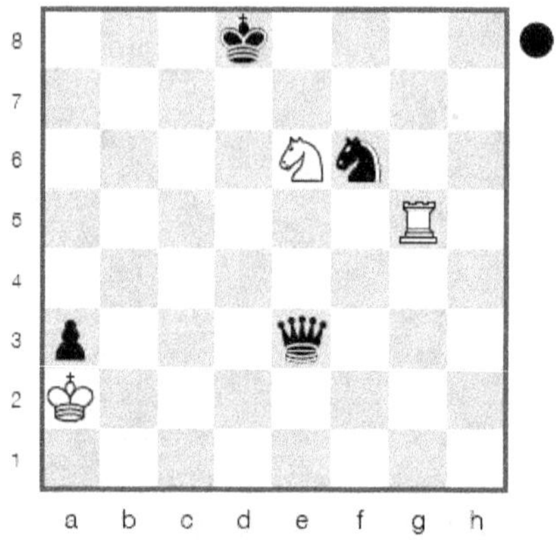

Qe3

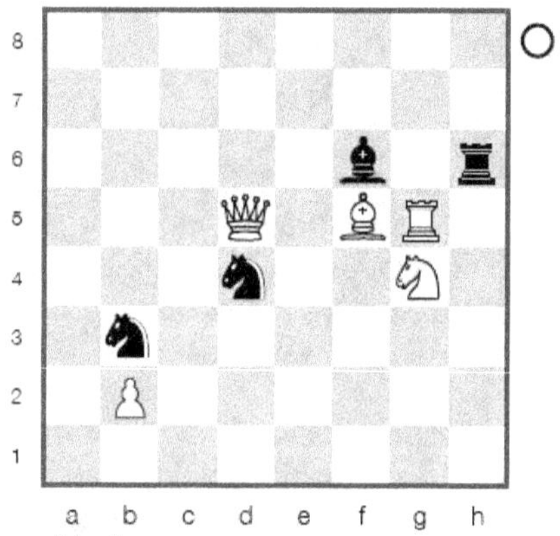

Ng4

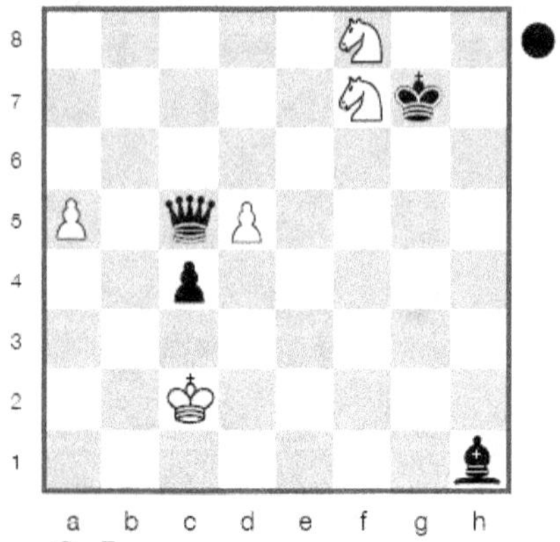

Qc5

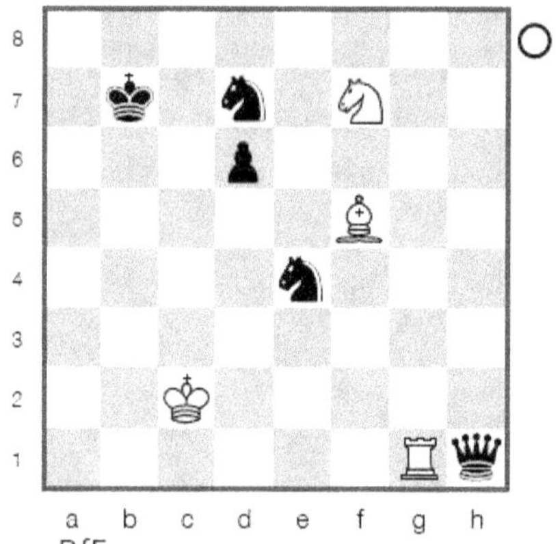

Bf5

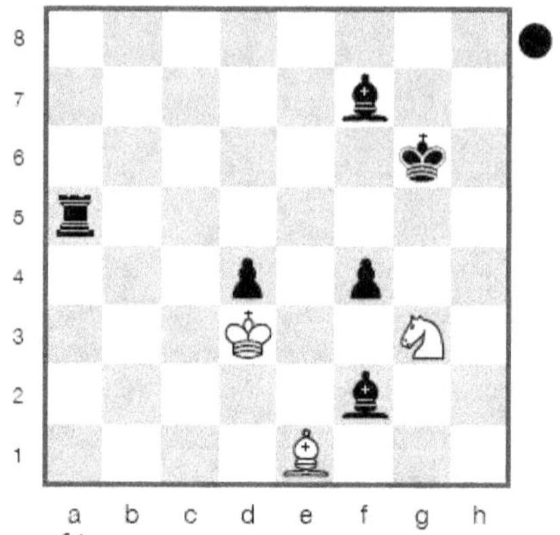

f4

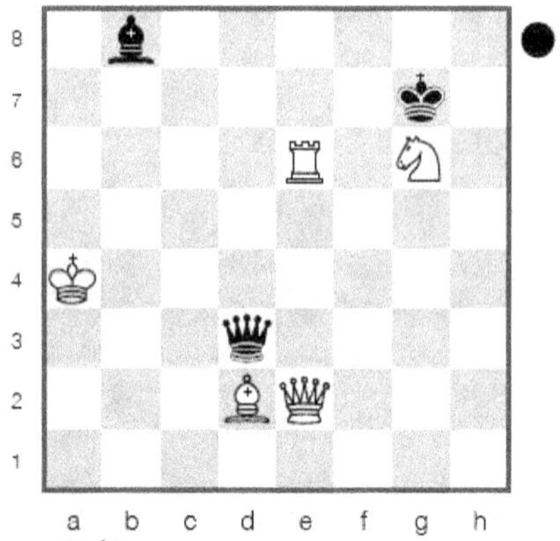

Qd3

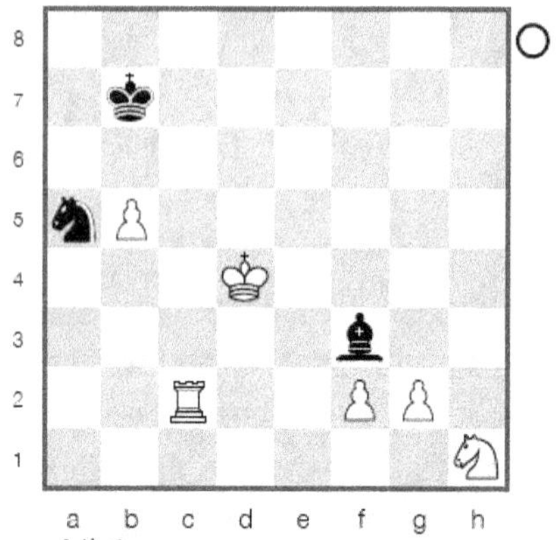

Nh1

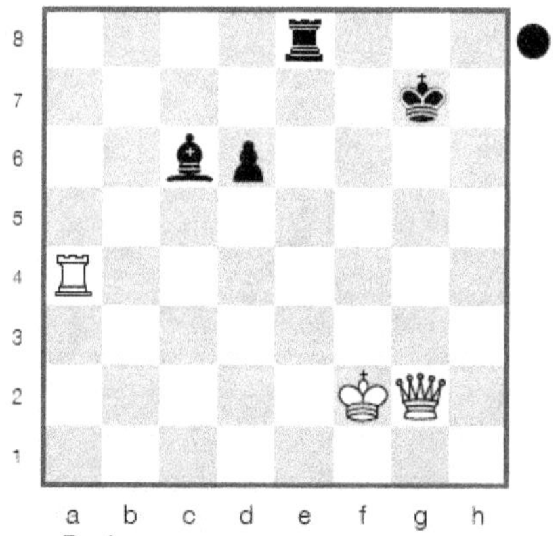

Bc6

The 3 Golden Rules

The three golden rules are commonly accepted as essential principles when starting a chess game. Following these rules will help prevent you from losing a game too quickly and increase your chances of having a better fight and enjoying the game.

1. Control The Center

The four squares at the very center of the board are often referred to as the 'power squares.' Occupying or reaching these squares with your pieces maximizes their effectiveness and activity.

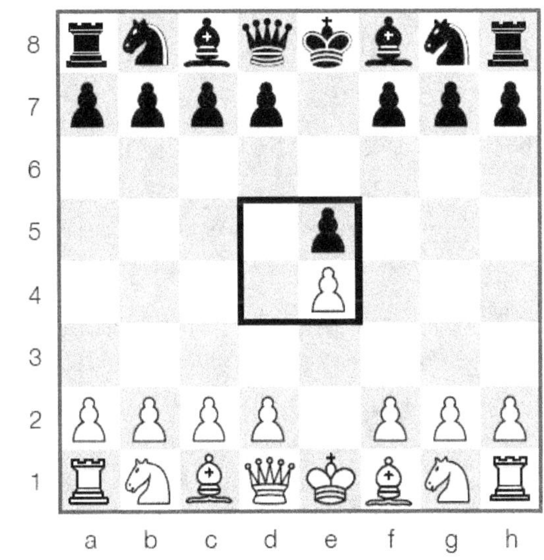

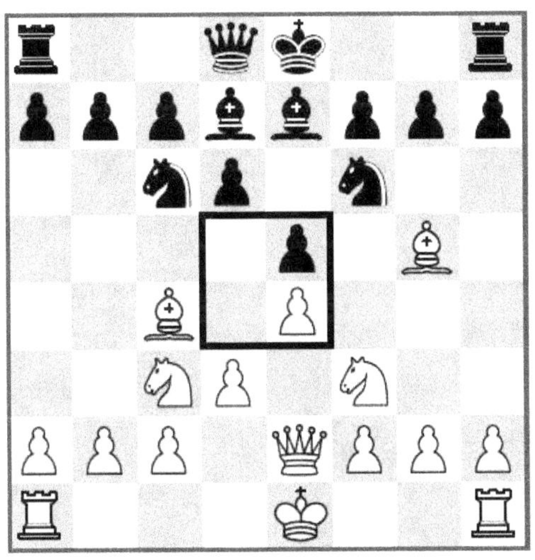

2.   Activate your pieces

Take a look at the Knights and Bishops; they have all moved from their original squares. This is what we refer to as 'activating' your pieces. In other words, your pieces are becoming more useful.

3. Getting your King Safe

After deploying your pieces into the center of the board, you will need to ensure the safety of your King to prevent it from being easily attacked. This is where Castling comes into play. Castling not only places the King in a safer position but also brings a Rook out of its corner. Castling will be explained in details in a next chapter.

Hanging Piece

Capturing the opponent's pieces is not only a rewarding but an essential strategy to secure victory in a game of Chess. When an opponent's piece is within your reach and lacks any form of defense, you should capture it promptly. In Chess terminology, a piece without protection and left vulnerable to capture is commonly referred to as a "Hanging Piece" or an "Unprotected Piece." In the following puzzles, your objective is to identify Hanging Pieces and execute their capture !

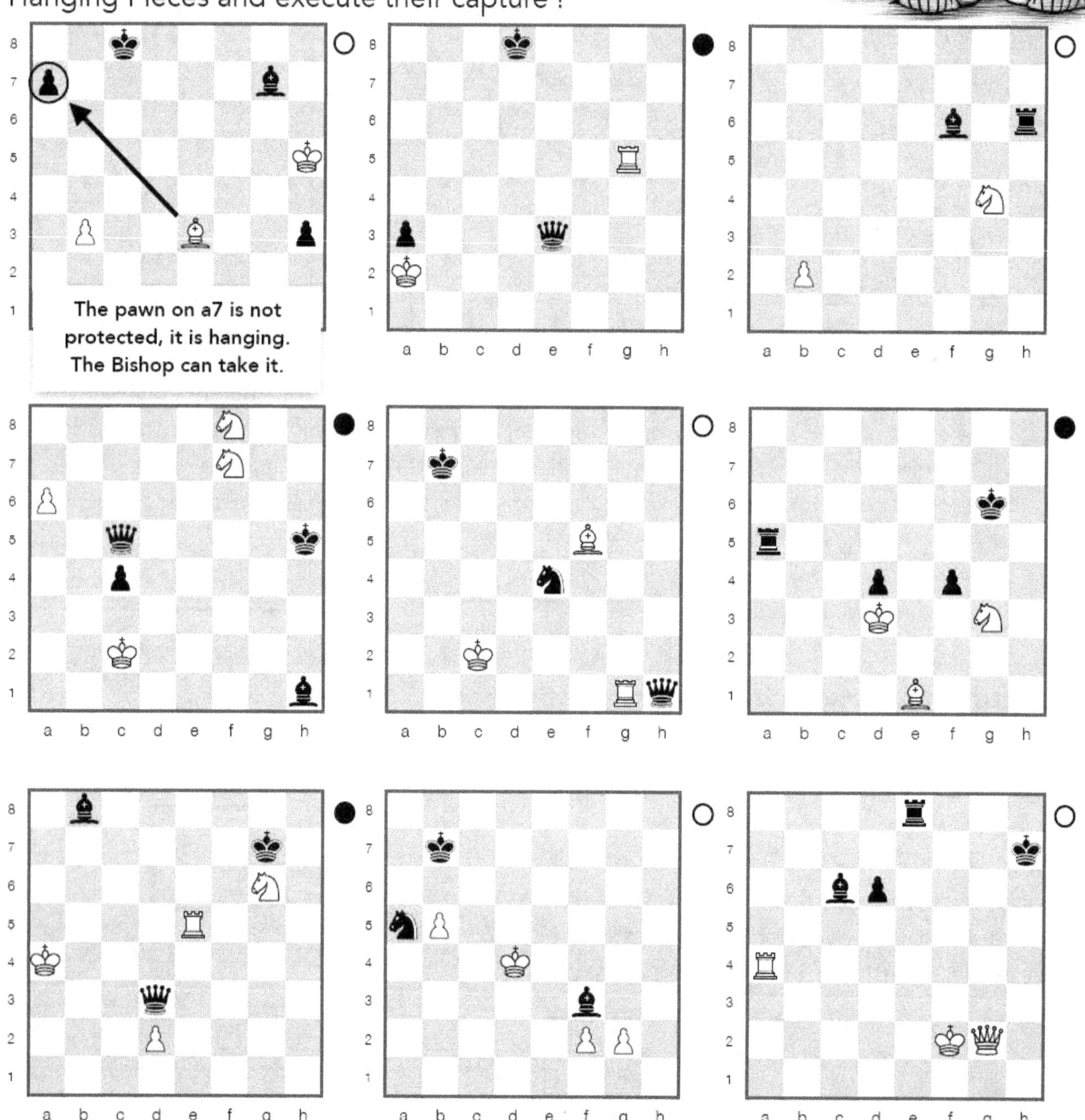

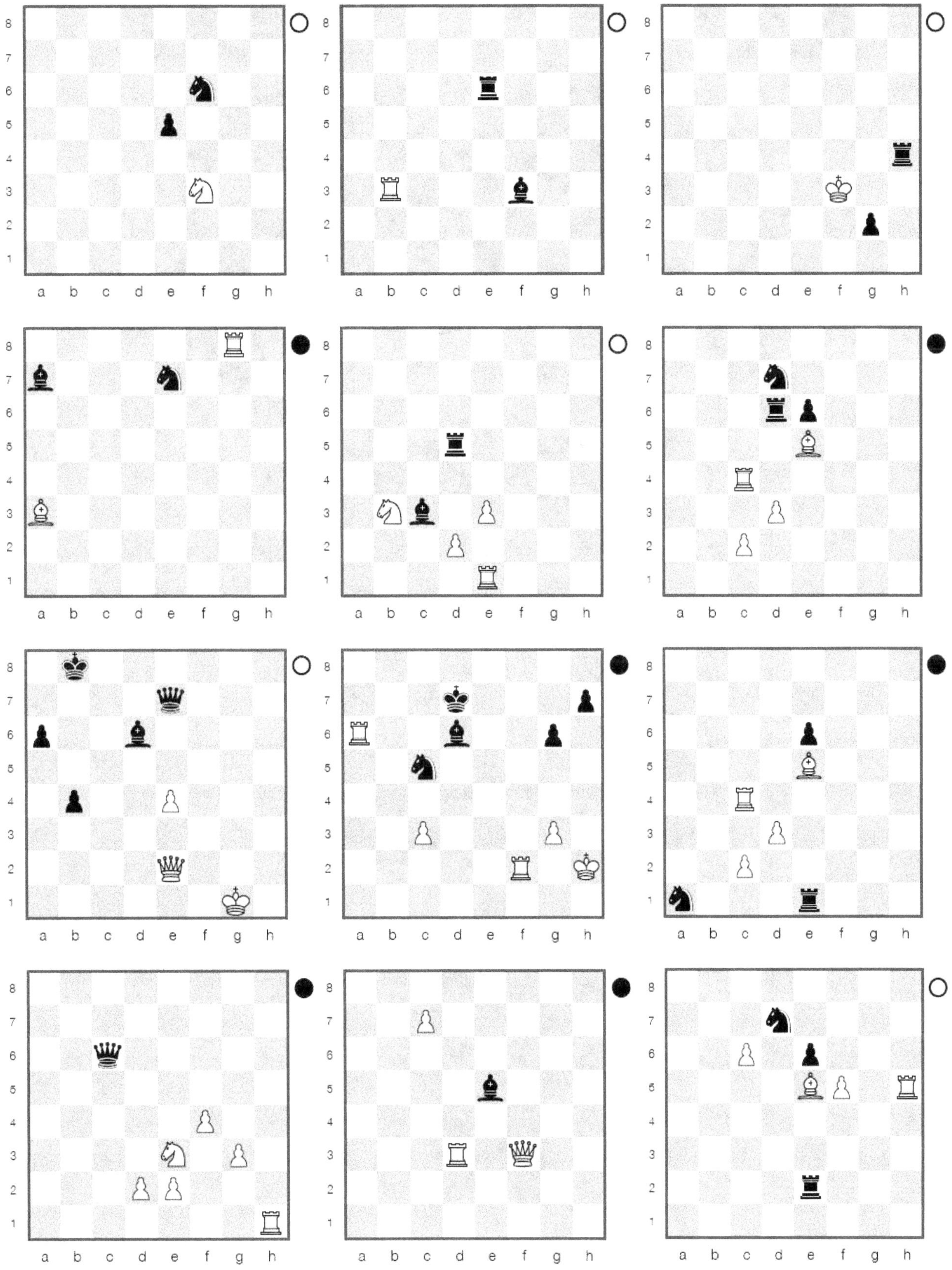

Capture
Award

Attacking

In Chess, an attack means 'threatening to capture' an opponent's piece. It is a fundamental aspect of the game, aimed at gaining a material advantage or weakening the opponent's position. Effective attacks can also expose the King, a crucial objective in chess. Attacks can be operated by any piece toward any opponent's piece. An attack on a King is called "Check".

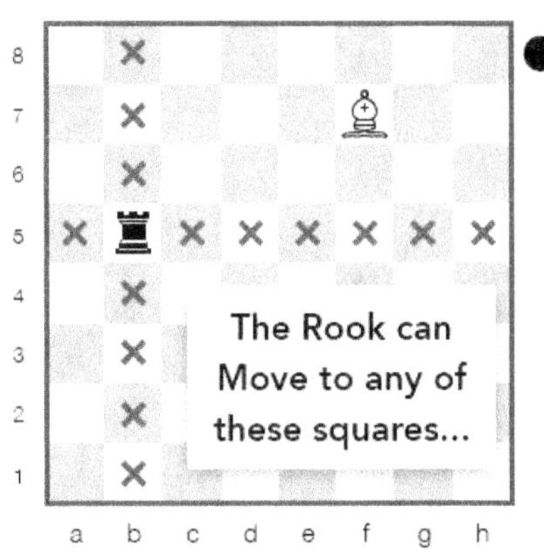

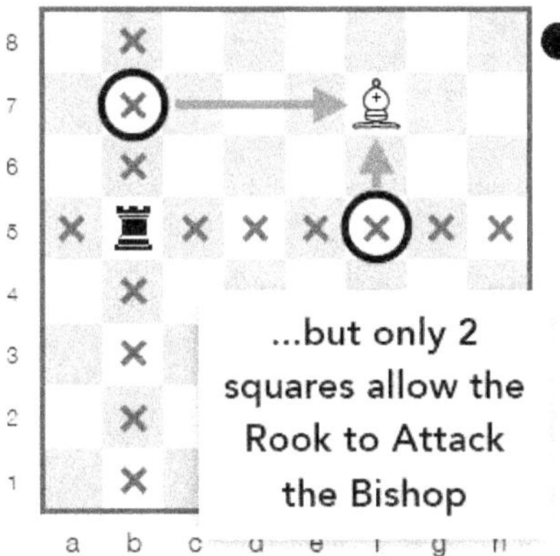

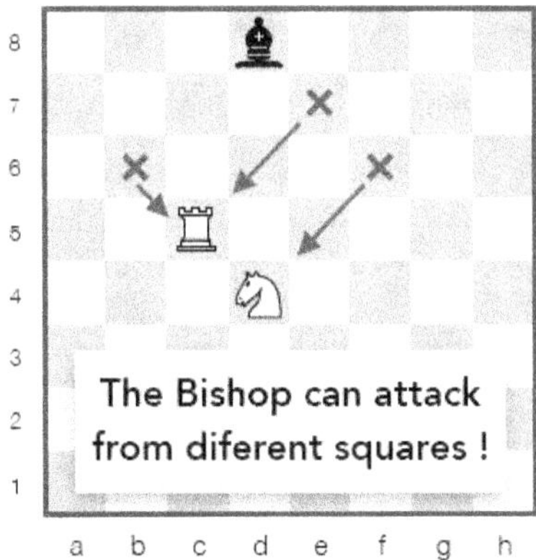

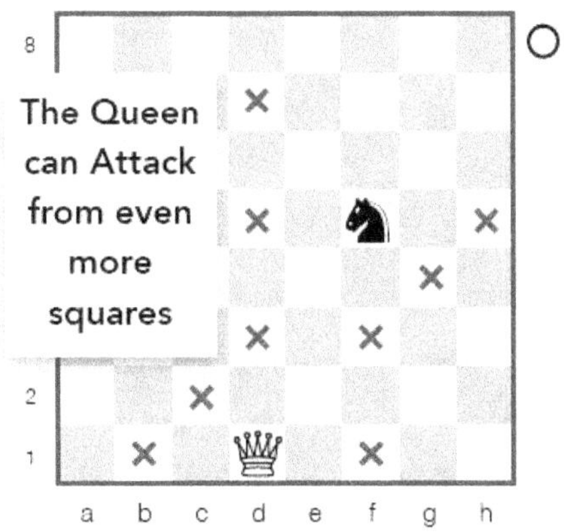

The Queen is the most powerful Attacker

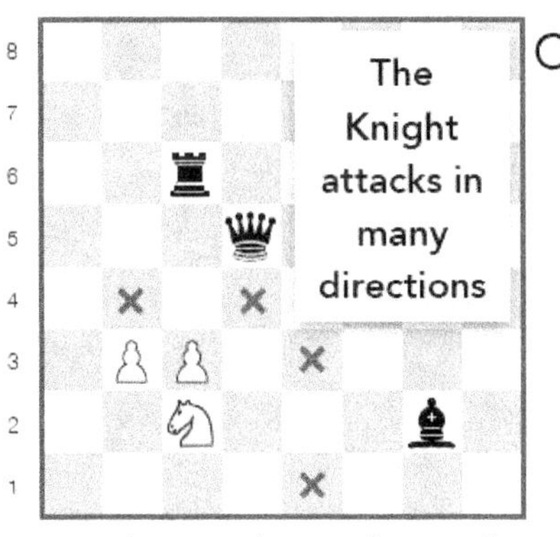

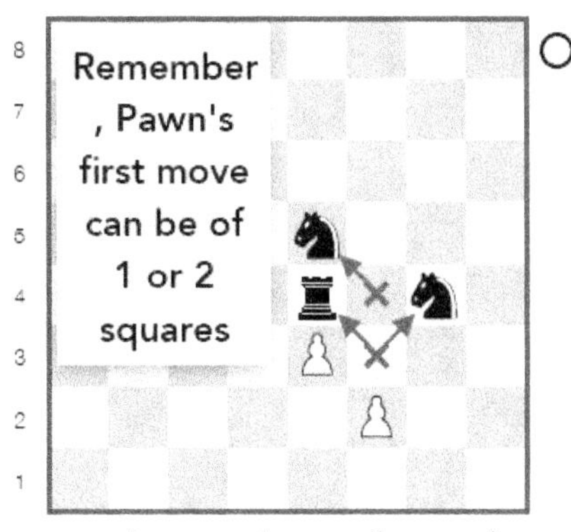

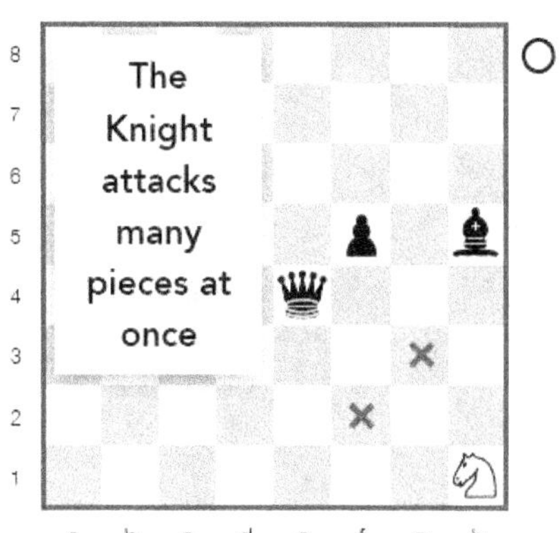

Attacking Puzzles

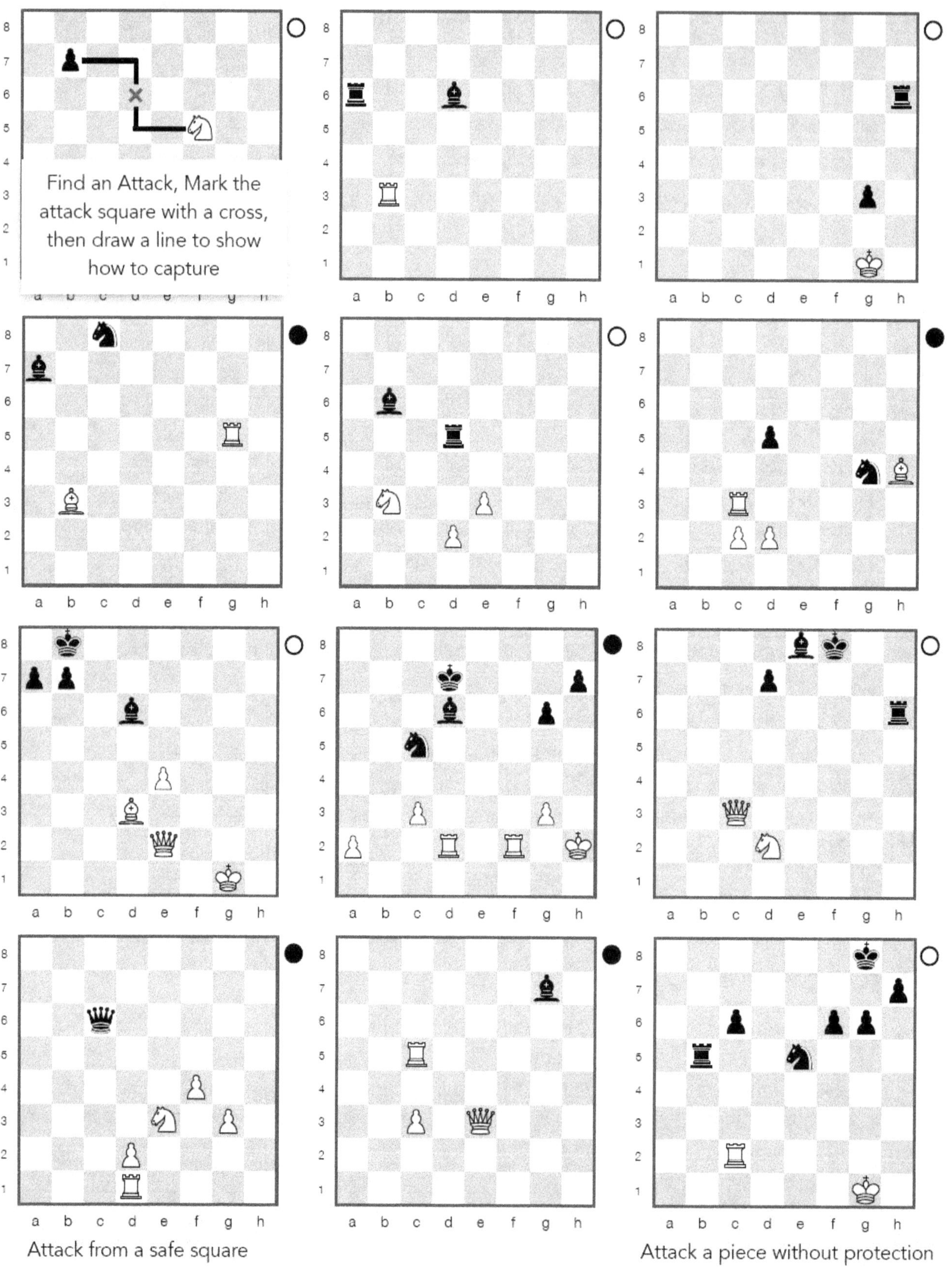

Attacking Puzzles

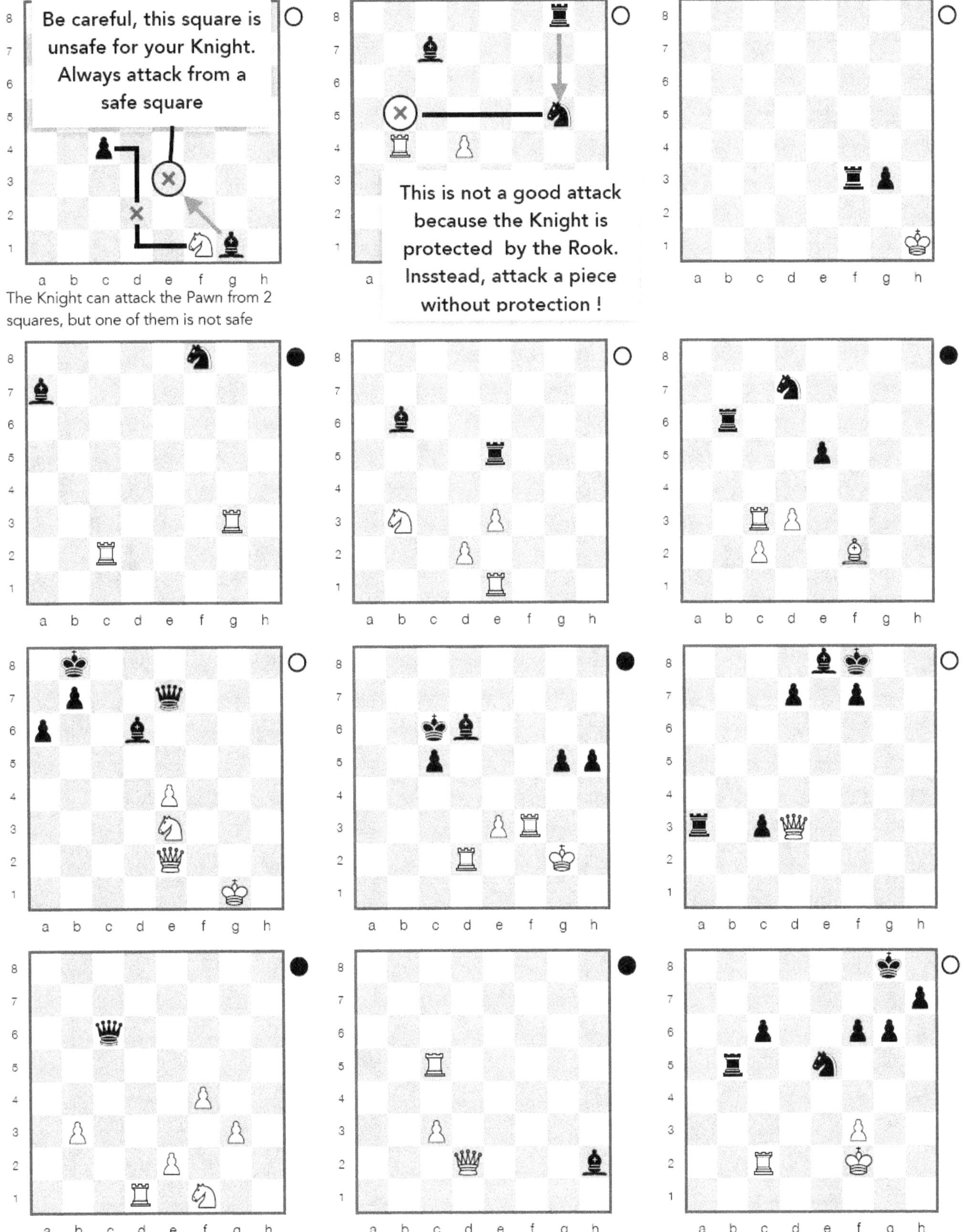

Attacking the King (Check)
From a safe square !

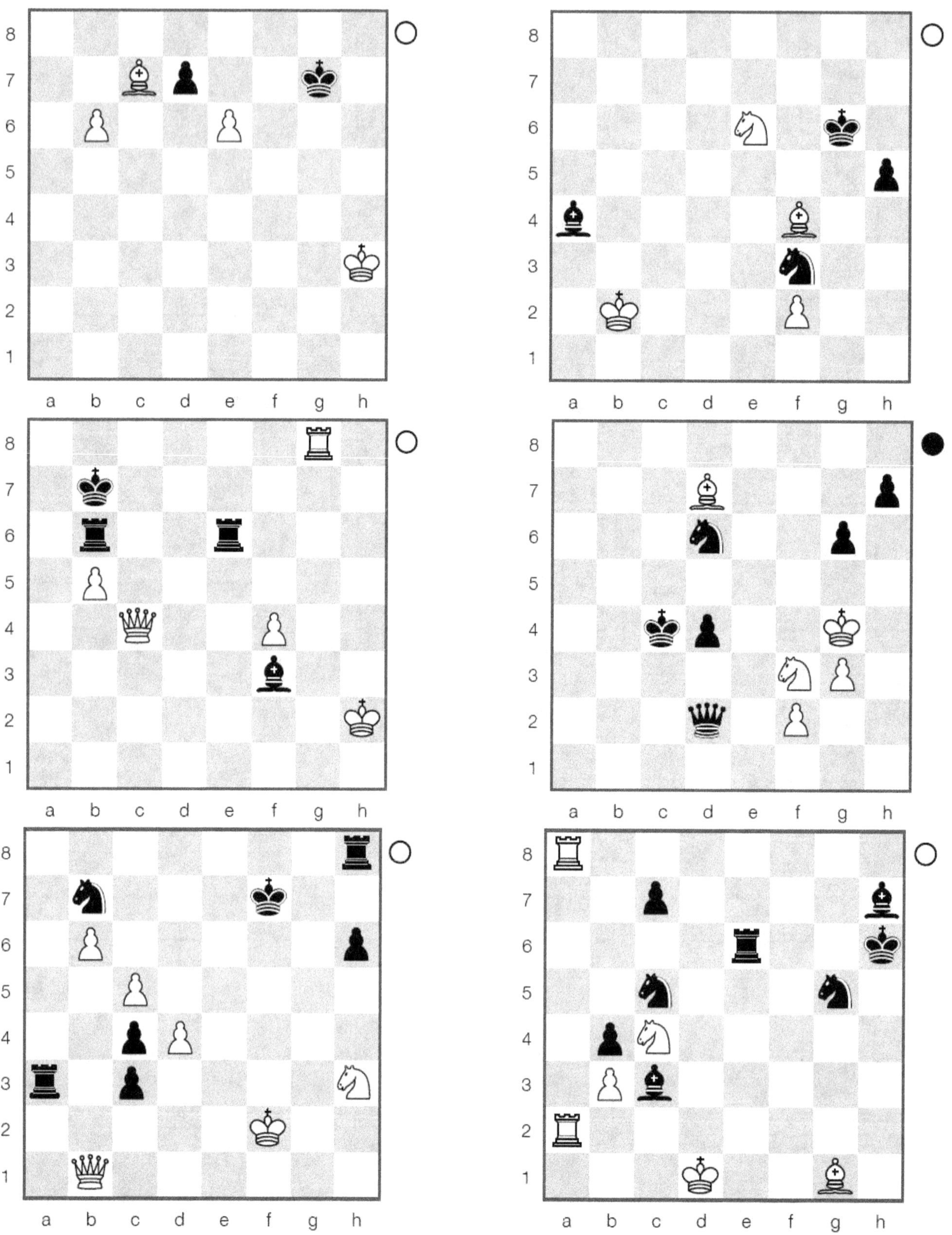

Your first game online !

As a kid, it is not always granted to have someone of your level to play with. In the mid 1980's it was a problem to me; my parents were not always available (nor interested) for a game with me.
But then came a surprise. I received an electronic Chess board for Saint-Nicolas. It was such a new technology at that time. From that day I could play with someone whenever I wanted. That someone was the tiny computer embedded in the board. For me it was a game changing.

Nowadays, similar but much more powerful computers are within our mobile phones, but wait...Now there is much more on internet, such as communities of players to talk to, news about top tournaments and champions, platforms to play against other online players (there is always someone waiting to play with), online tournaments or robots (these never sleep!).

Online Chess platforms also offer teaching classes in order to improve your Chess skills, and many more tools.
Here is a list of the best platforms I have come through, and there is no doubt you will find satisfaction in any of them.

Lichess.org: Completely free, very popular and lots of players connected. I suggest you to **create your free account today** and just start playing while you keep on reading this book.
Chess.com: Great community, usesful tools if you want to progress. They even organise big tournaments.
Chess24.com: Excellent platform to play, learn and follow Chess News of the world.
Chesskid.com: The platform for kids and coaches.
Chessclub.com: ICC, Internet Chess Club, is a very famous club online.

Fide.com: The International Chess Federation
Chess Federations by country: https://fide.com/directory/member-federations

Creating an Attack

Use the piece beside the board to create an attack

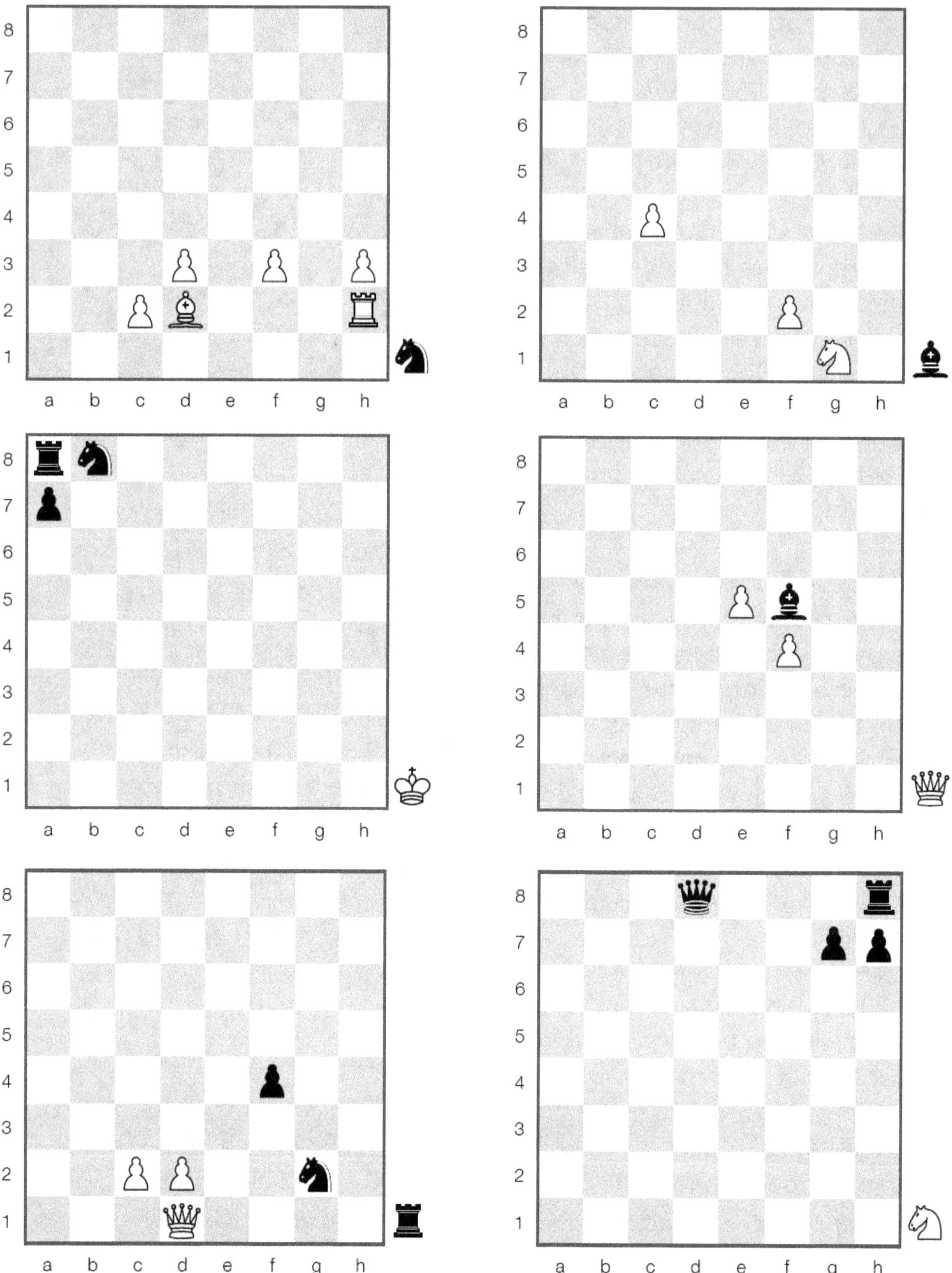

Attacking Puzzles

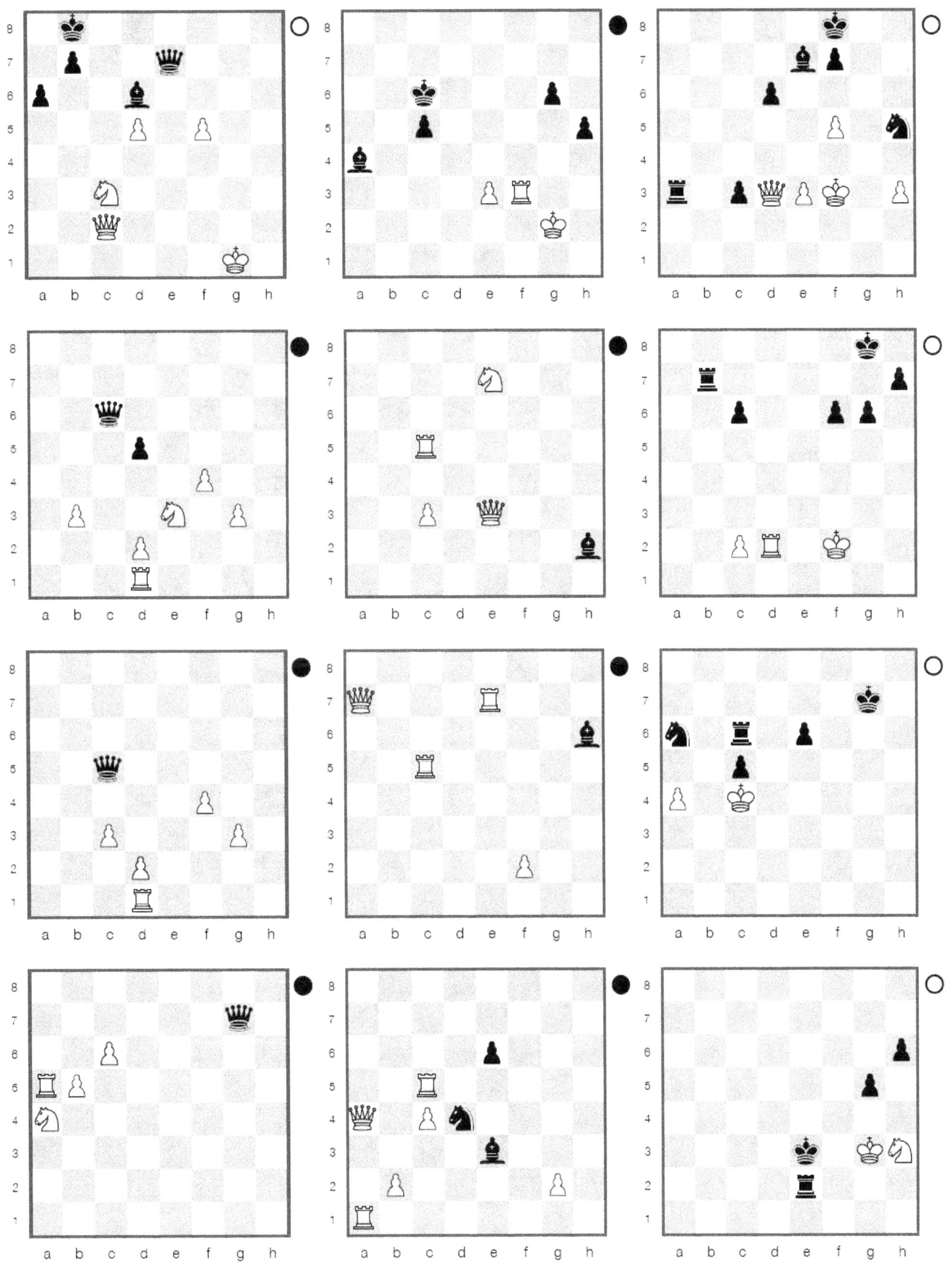

41

I CAN ATTACK

Defending

If you are under attack, you better defend
yourself or your piece will be captured.
In this chapter we will learn the different ways to
defend our pieces.
In the examples below, the black player just
played and moved its black Rook to b7
to attack the white Bishop. Now it is
white's turn to play; Let's see what the
white player can do to defend its Bishop !

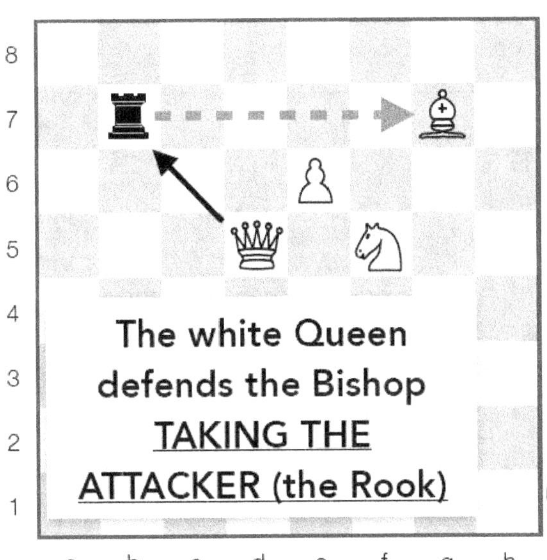

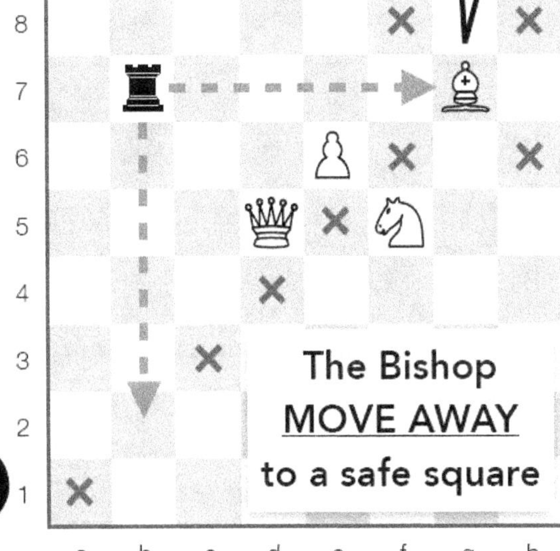

TA   MO

PRO   BLO

Defending / Taking the Attacker (TA)   Puzzles

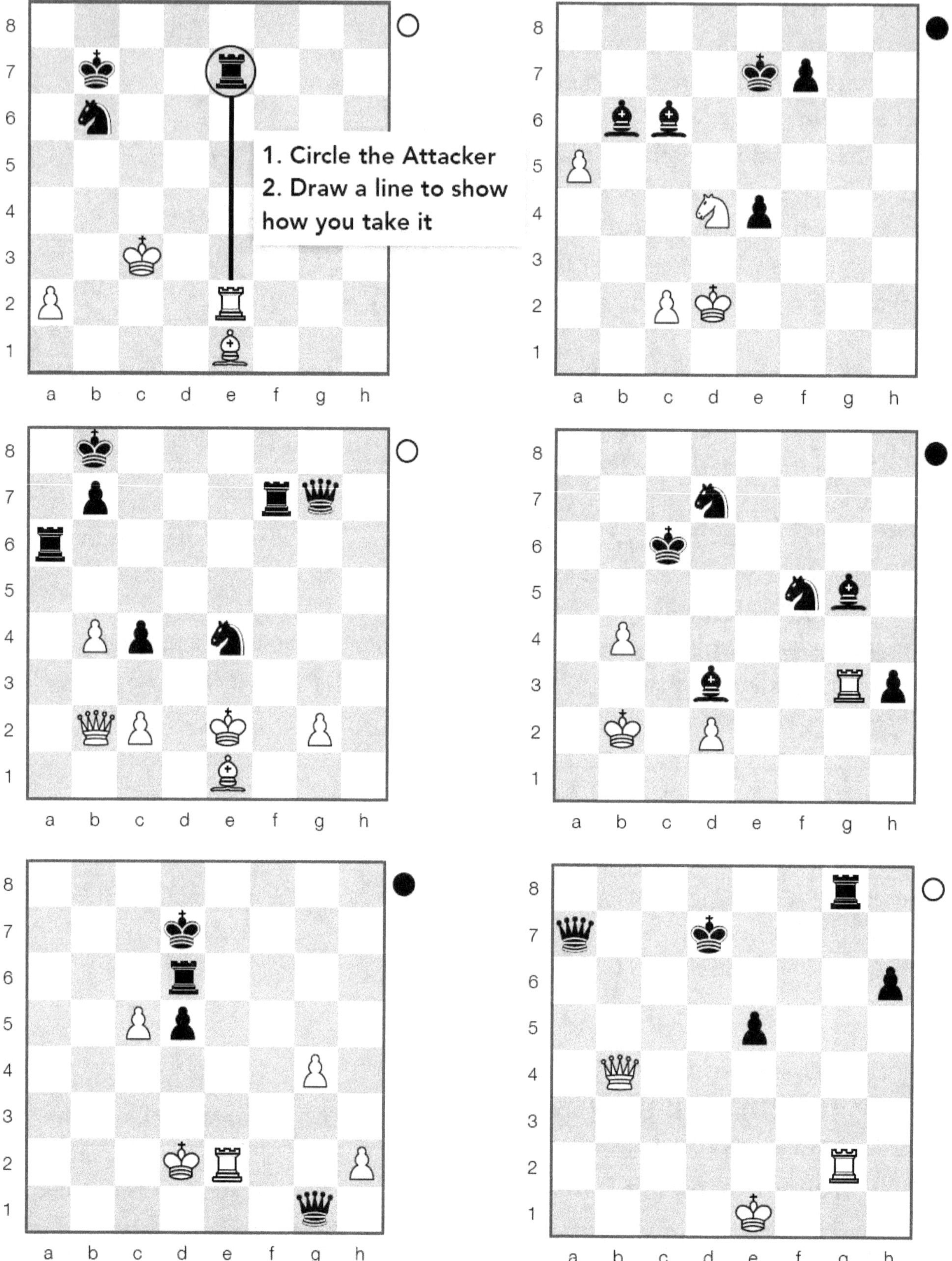

Defending / Move Away (MO)   Puzzles

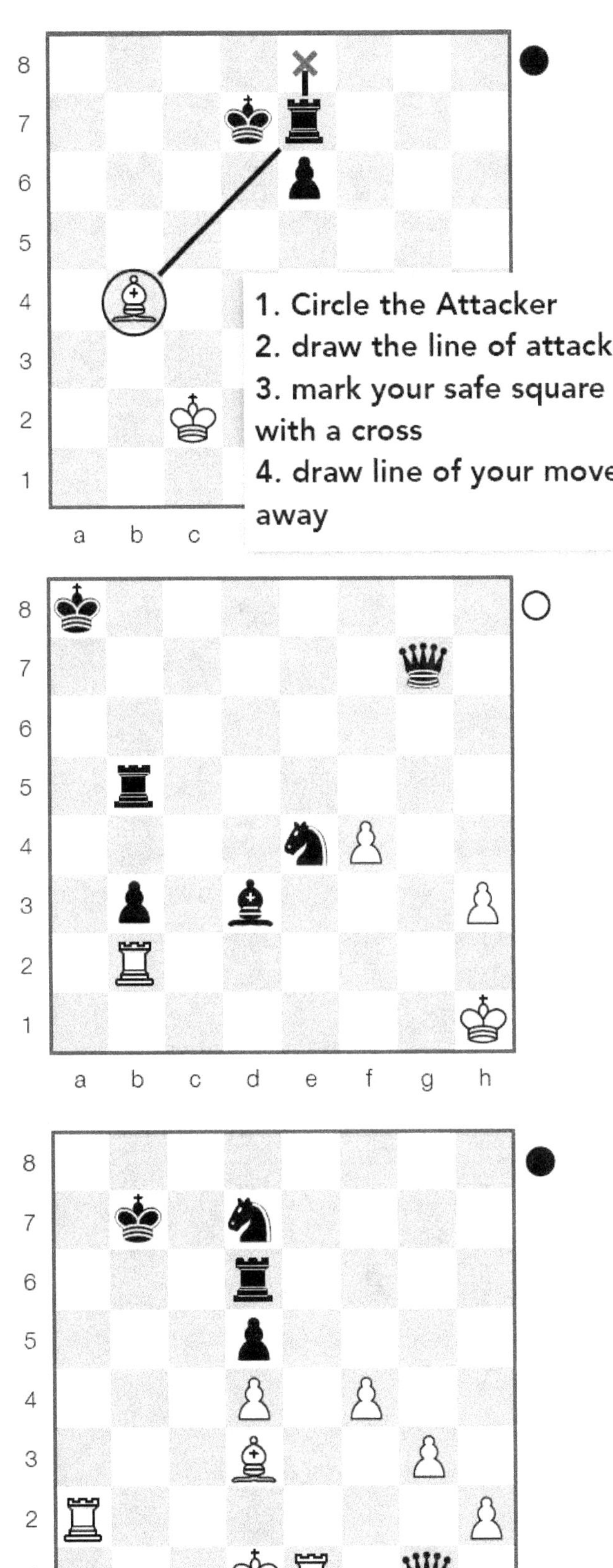

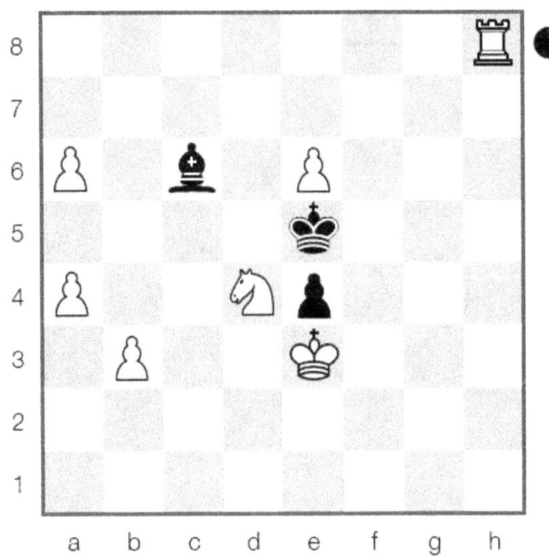

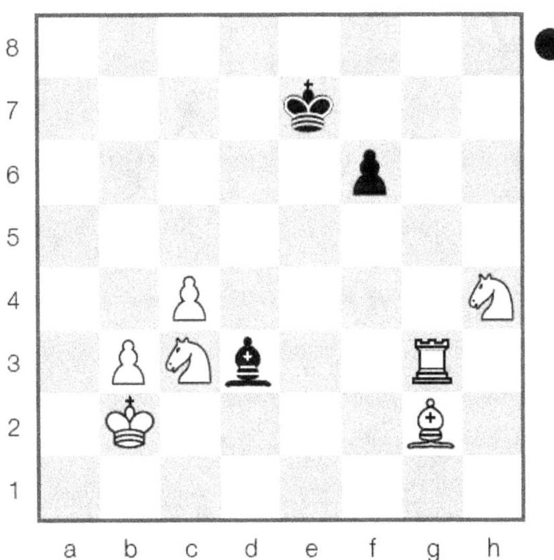

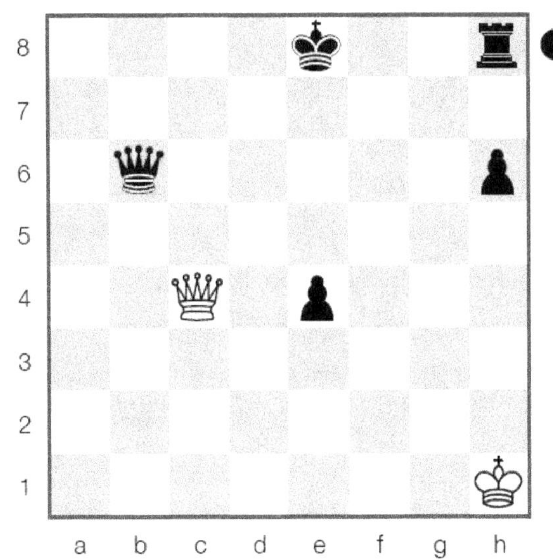

Defending / Protect (PRO)   Puzzles

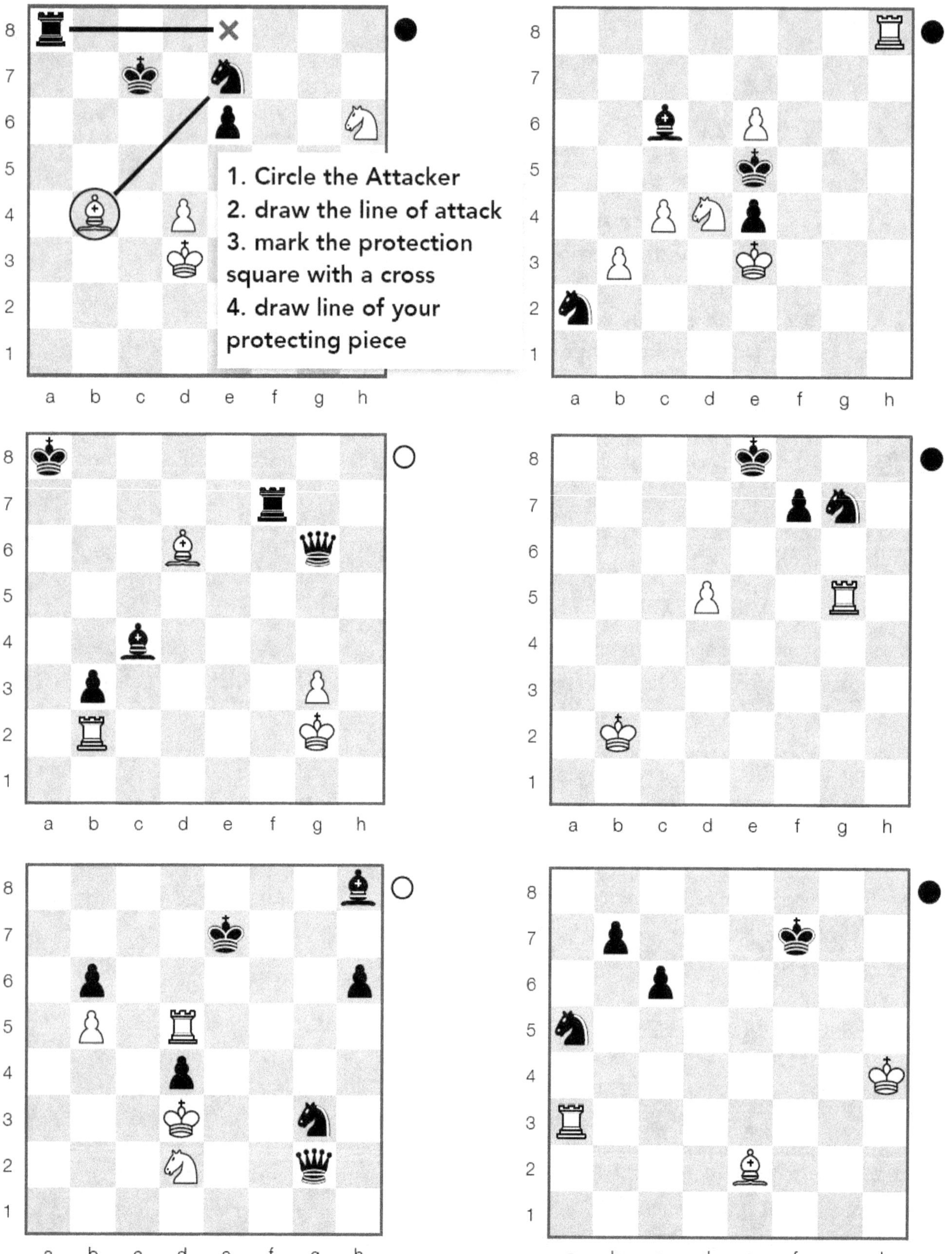

Defending / Block (BLO)   Puzzles

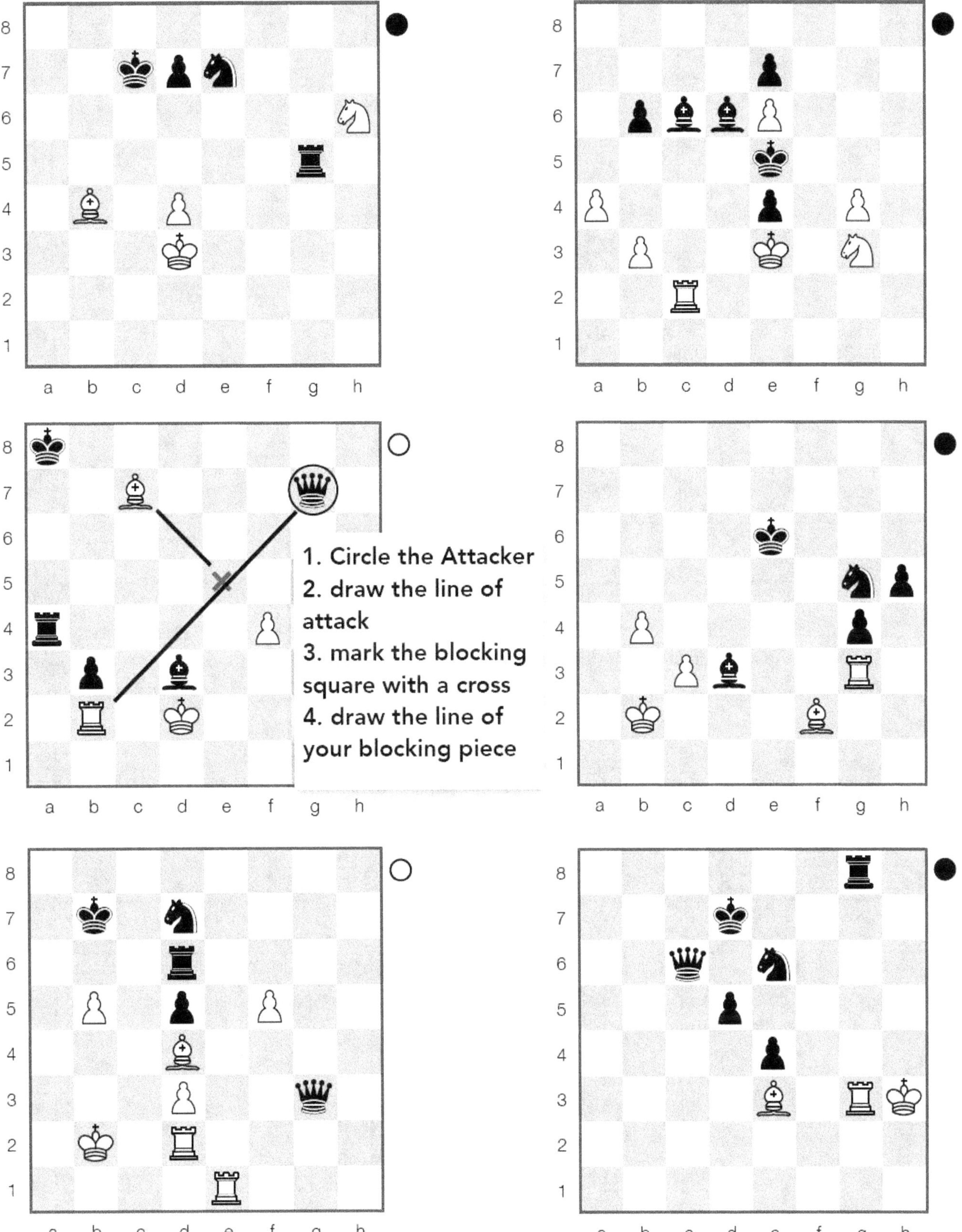

47

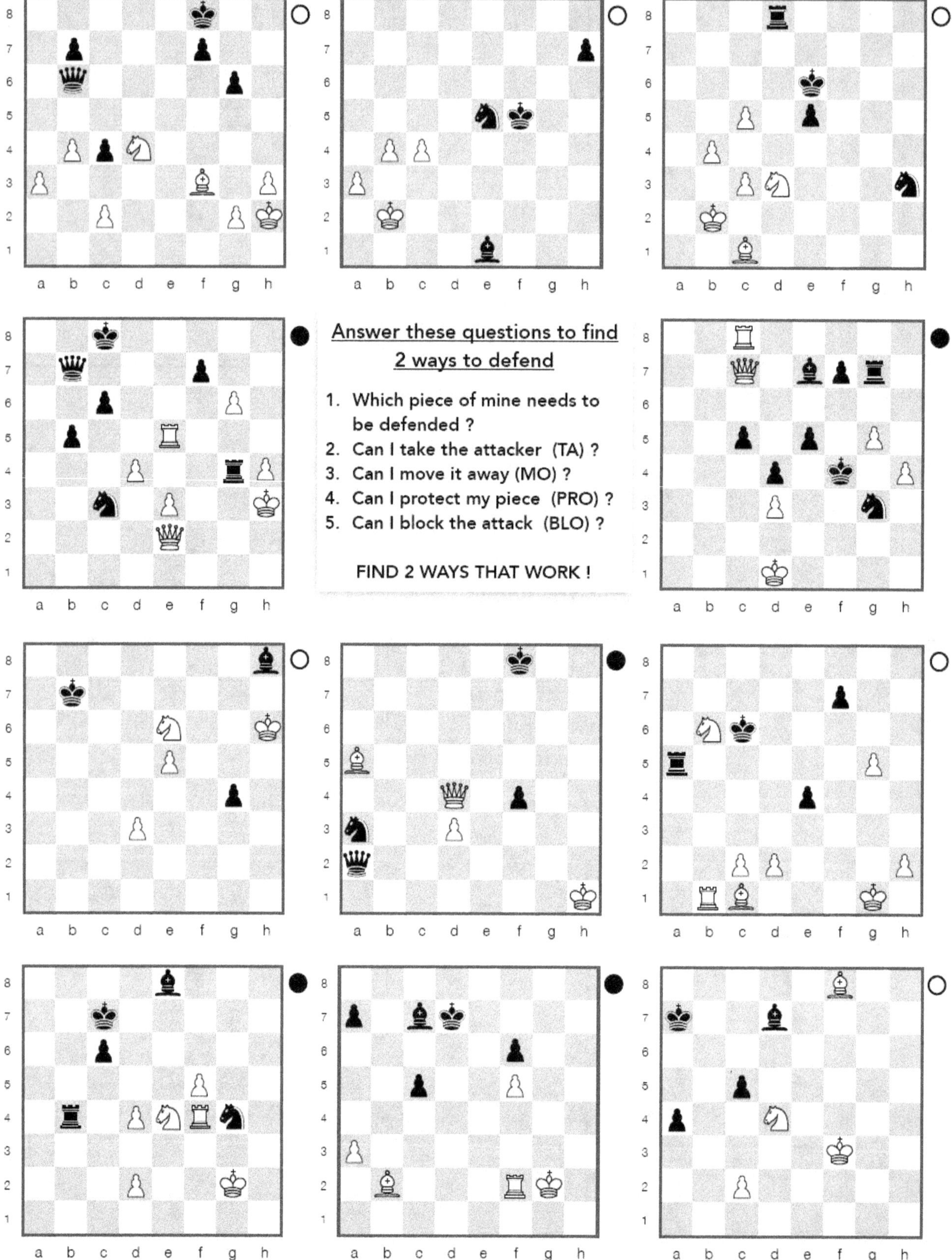

Answer these questions to find
2 ways to defend

1. Which piece of mine needs to
   be defended ?
2. Can I take the attacker (TA) ?
3. Can I move it away (MO) ?
4. Can I protect my piece (PRO) ?
5. Can I block the attack (BLO) ?

FIND 2 WAYS THAT WORK !

Check & Out of Check

The King is 'Check' when it is under attack by one of the opponent's pieces.

When your King is in Check, you have to defend it immediately by taking it out of check.

There are several ways to get your

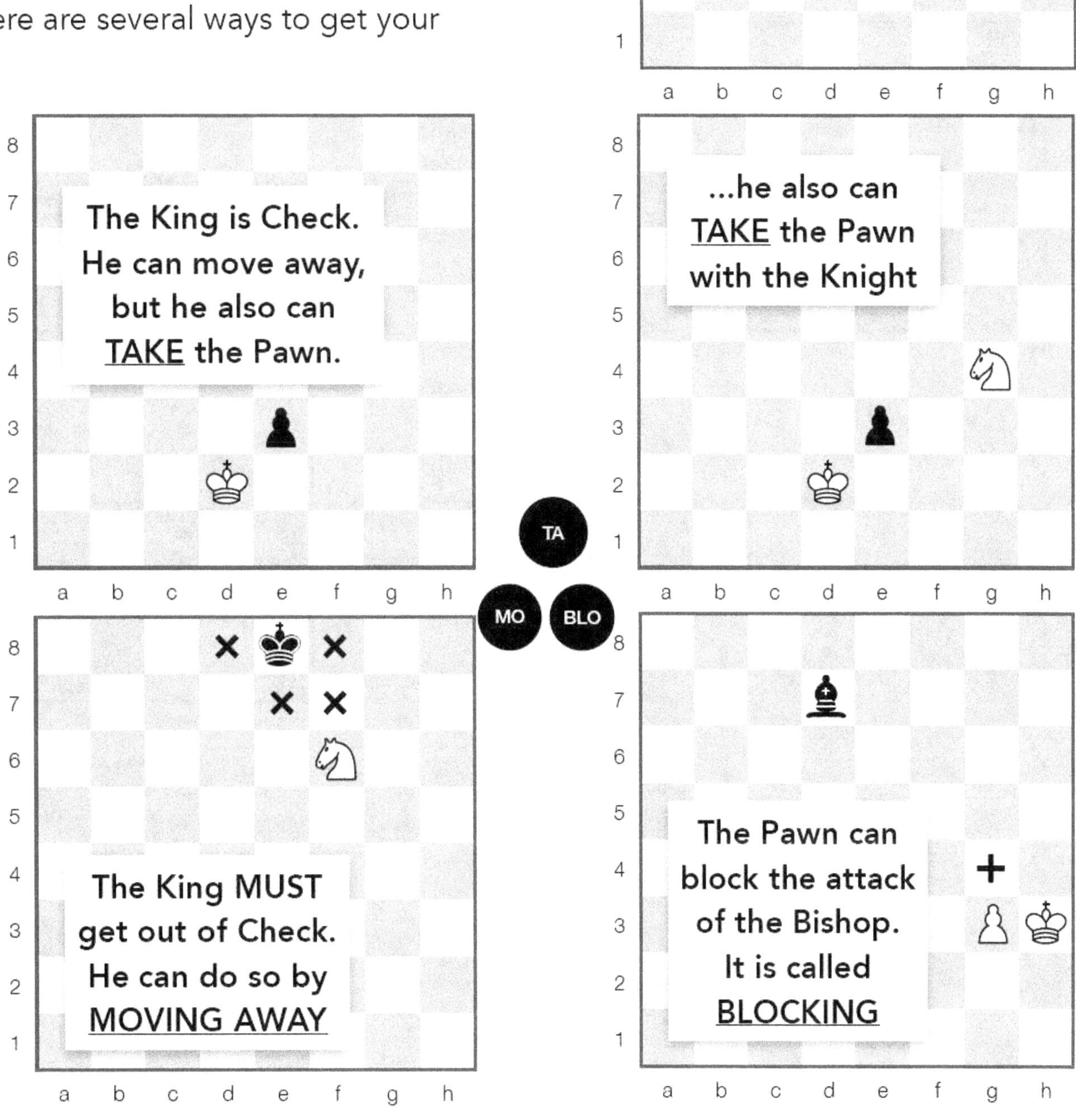

49

Get out of Check

Puzzles

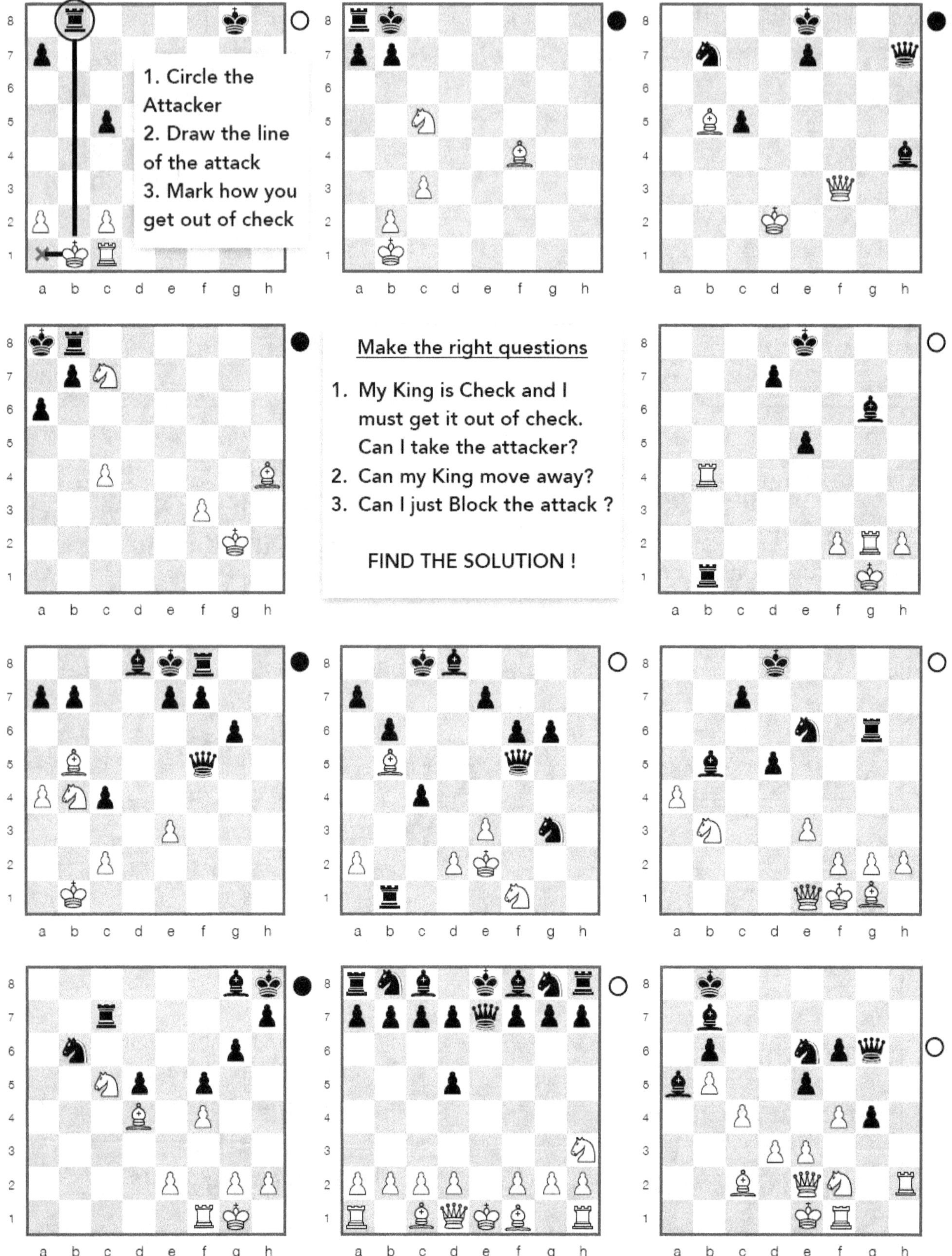

Castling

Castling is a Defensive move that involves 2 pieces at once: the King and 1 Rook.

What is it used for? In a single move, your King moves to safety and 1 Rook is activated ! It's a clever move!

You can castle on the King's side (short castle), or on the Queen's side (long castle)

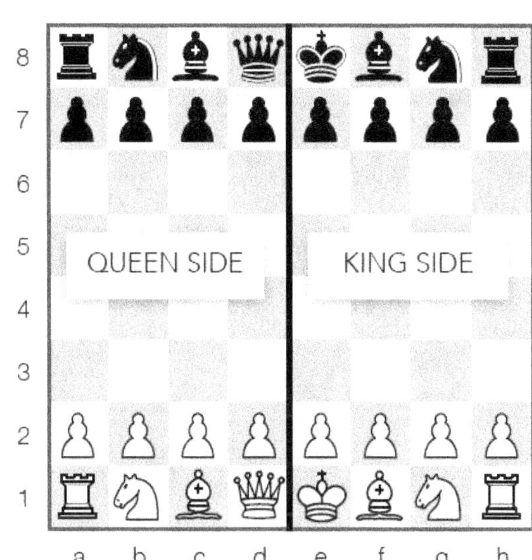

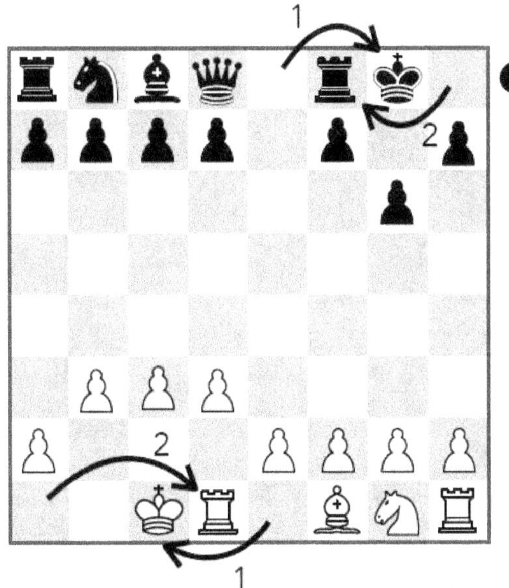

Black have just castled on the King's side: first, the King moved two squares toward the Rook, and then the Rook jumped to the other side of the King

White have castled on the Queen's side: the King moved two squares Toward the Rook, and then the Rook jumped to the other side of the King

1. To Castle, squares between the King and the Rook must be empty

4 Rules of Castling

2. To Castle, the King and the Rook should have never moved. Never.

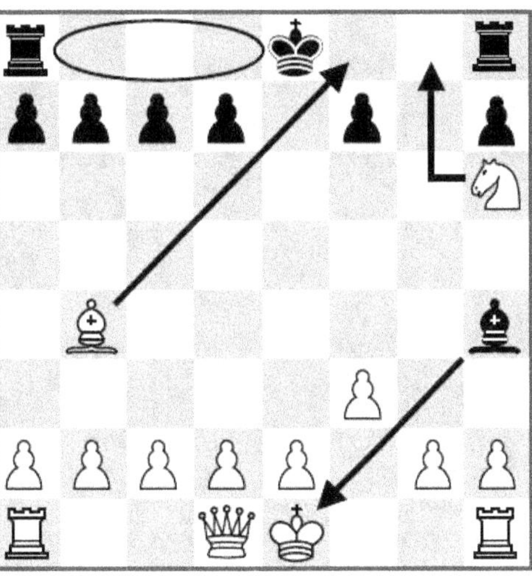

3. To Castle, squares where the King passes or ends should not be under attack

4. If the King is in Check, you cannot Castle !

Castling Practice

May Black castle queenside? Yes / no

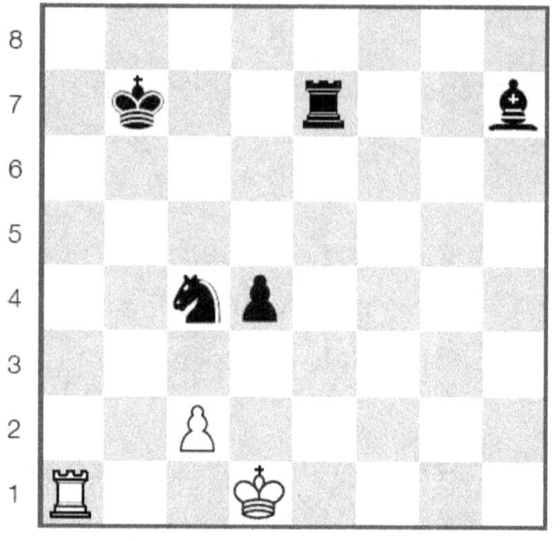

May White castle kingside? Yes / no

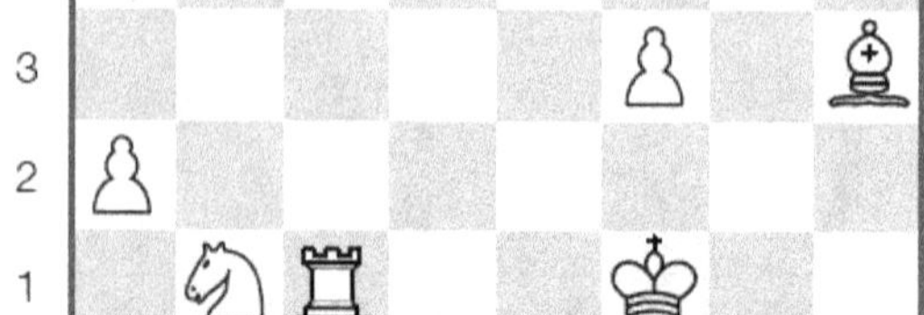

May White castle kingside? Yes / no

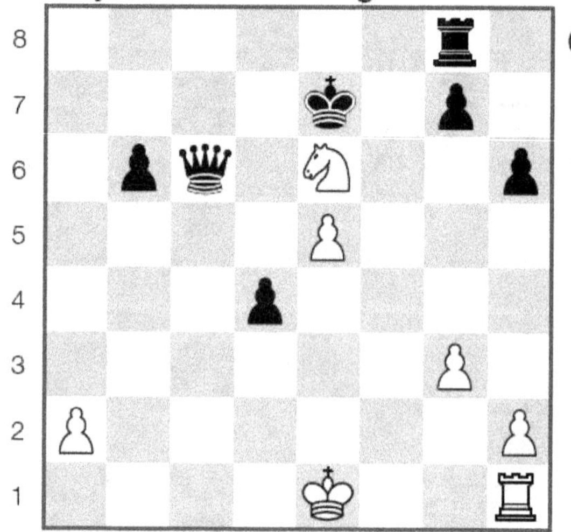

May White castle kingside? Yes / no

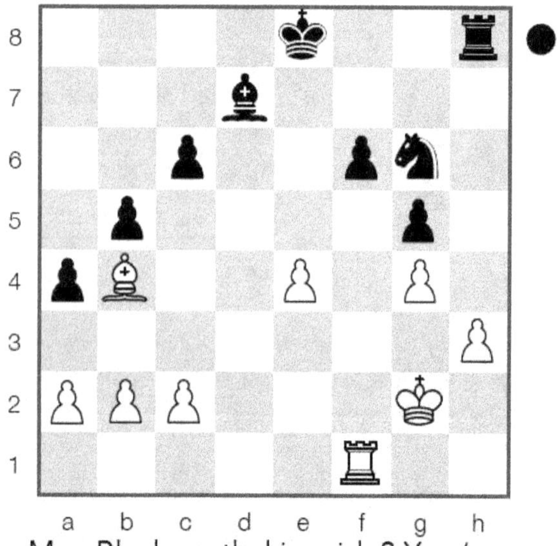

May Black castle kingside? Yes / no

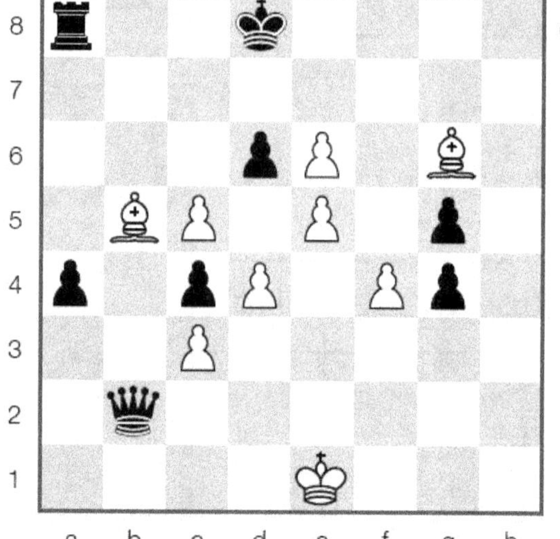

May Black castle queenside? Yes / no

Defending / Mix

Puzzles

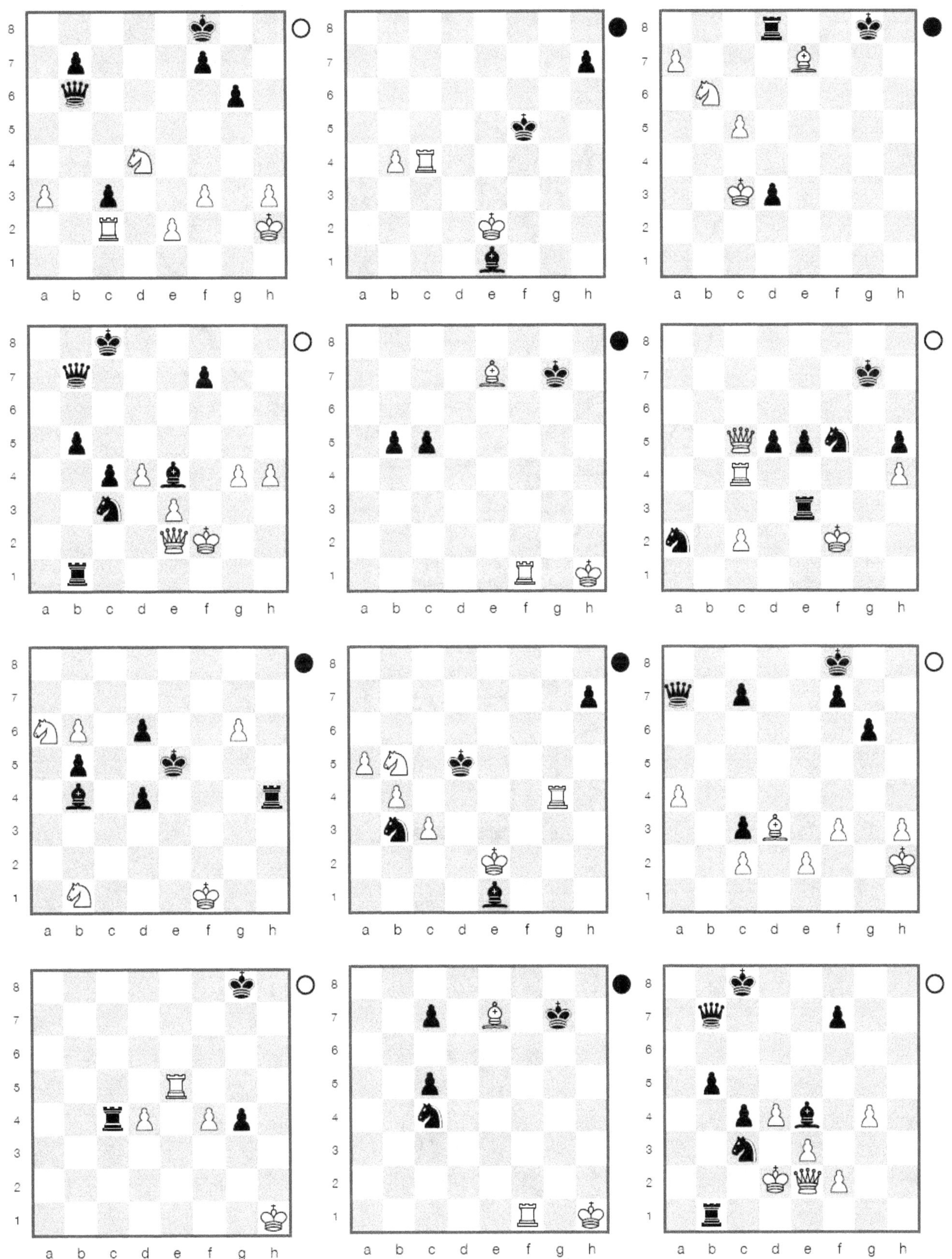

I CAN DEFEND

Checkmate

Chess is a battle between two armies led by their Kings. The objective of each army is to trap the opponent's King.
If a King is in Check, it must escape from Check. If it can't escape, we call it 'Checkmate,' and the game ends.

The first player to achieve Checkmate against the enemy's King wins the game!

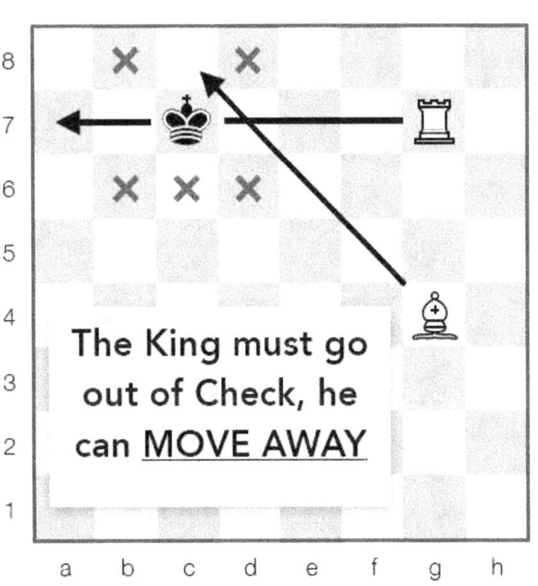

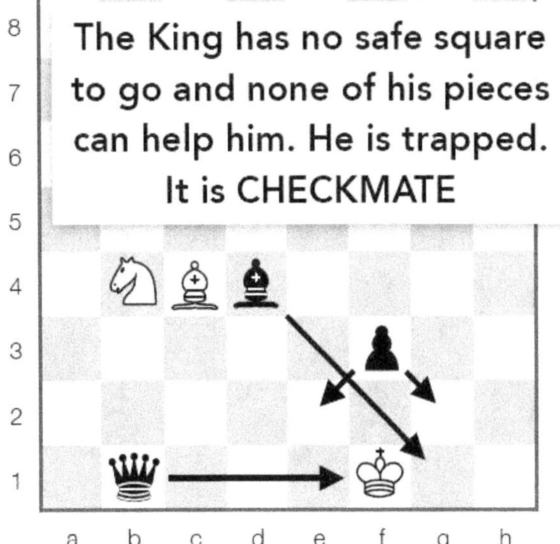

Checkmate with a Rook

Imagine you have a Rook, which is one of the powerful pieces on the board. Now, picture this: Your Rook is positioned in a way that it directly attacks your opponent's King, either from the same row or the same column. The opponent's King can't escape because your Rook covers all the squares it can move to. When your Rook creates this situation, and the opponent's King has no way to move to a safe square or capture your Rook, that's checkmate! It's a victory for you.

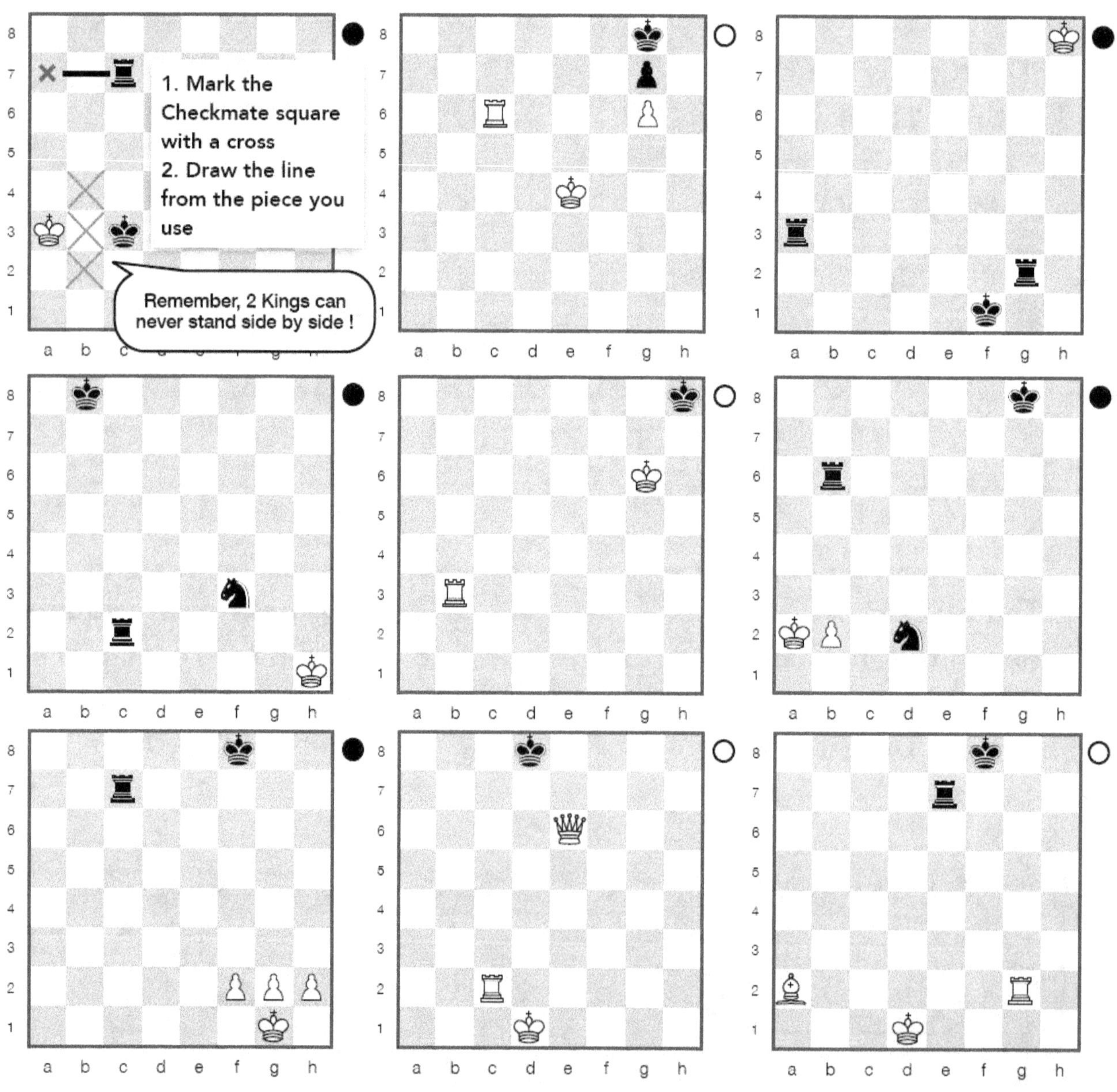

Checkmate with a Bishop

In order to use your Bishop to Checkmate the opponent's King, it is important to remind its way to move: diagonally. It can only go on squares with the same color as where it started. So, we should use our Bishop to control diagonal lines on the board. It's like a laser beam that goes diagonally in all directions. Bishop works best when it has friends like Pawns and other pieces. Together, they can protect each other and control more squares. Make sure your Bishop is not in danger from the other player's pieces.

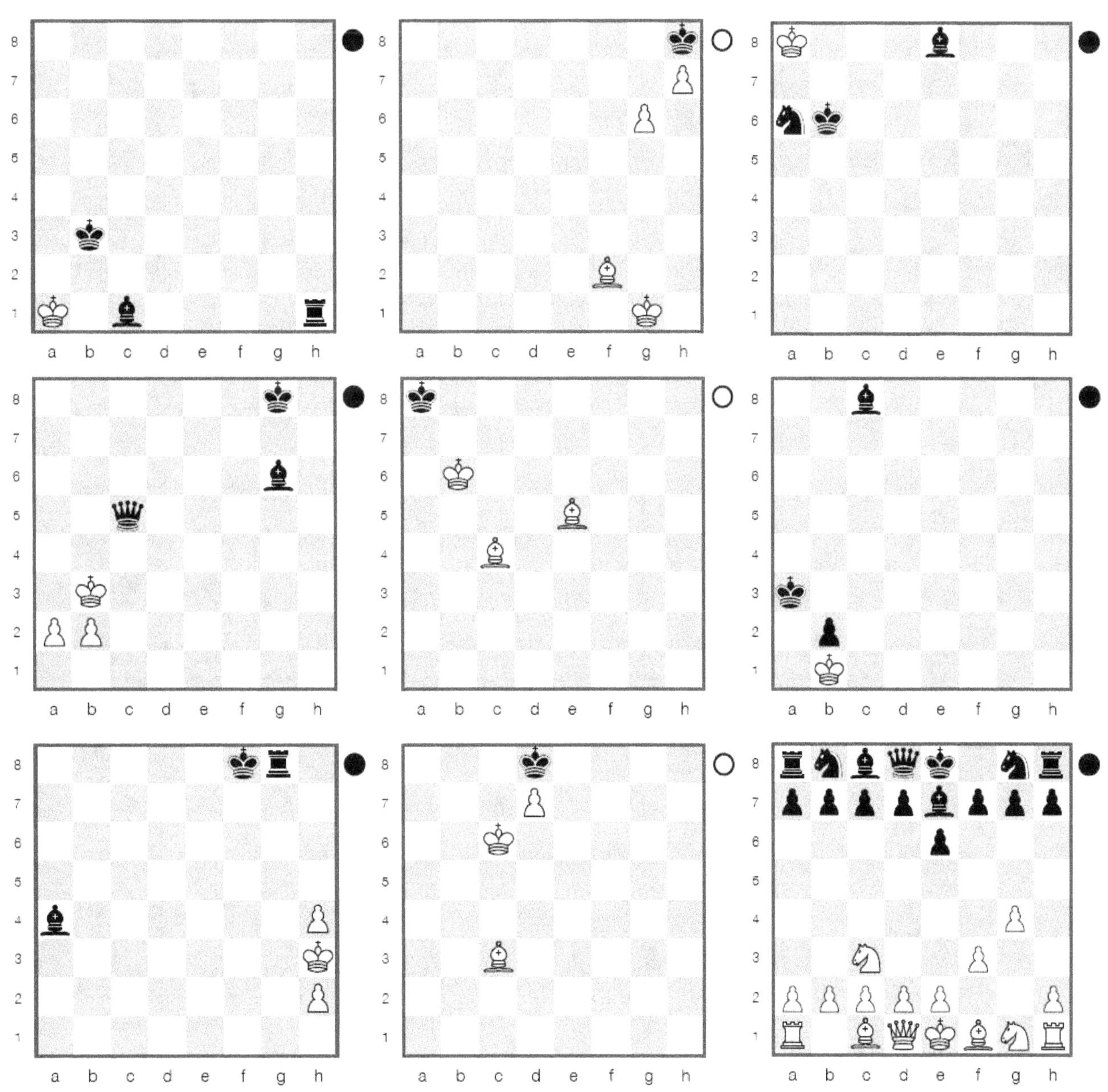

Checkmate with a Knight

The Knight is a remarkable chess piece that can be a stealthy weapon when it comes to delivering checkmate. You already have aknowledged the Knight has a unique 'L-shaped' move – two squares in one direction and then one square perpendicular to that. This special ability allows the Knight to jump over other pieces on the board, making it a tricky piece to predict. It's a unique and satisfying way to secure victory in chess by using the Knight's special movement.

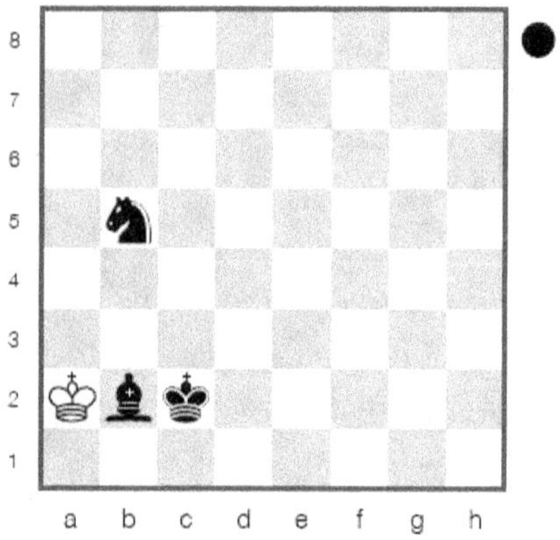

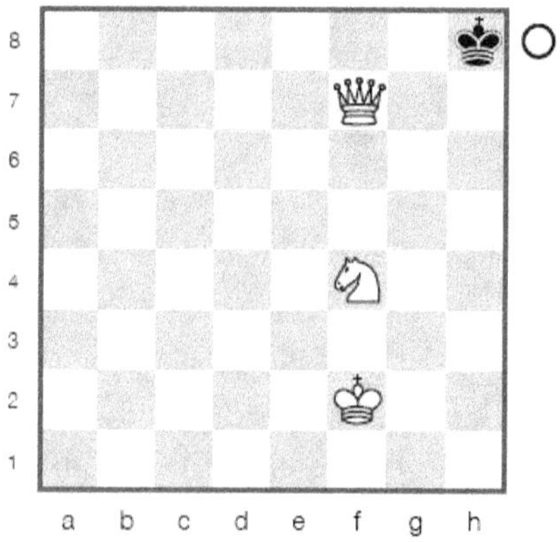

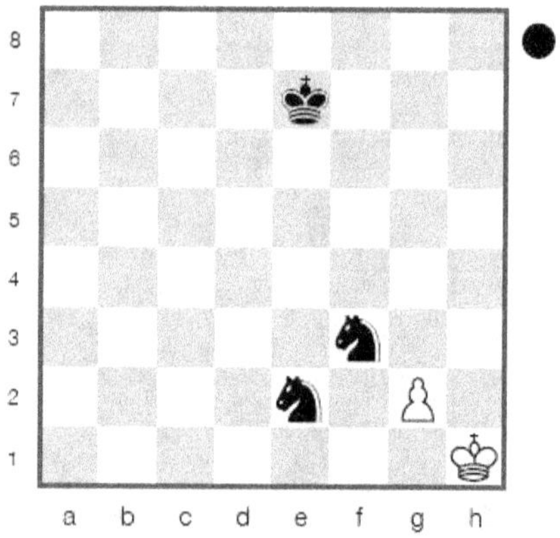

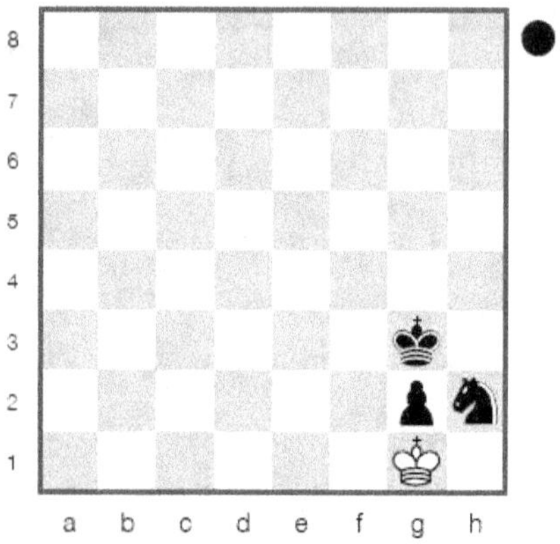

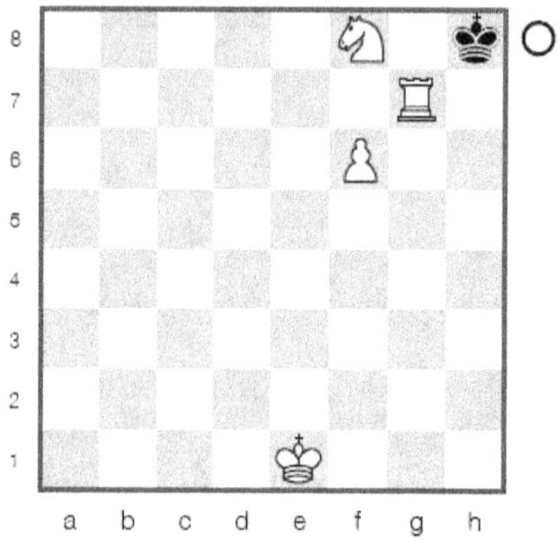

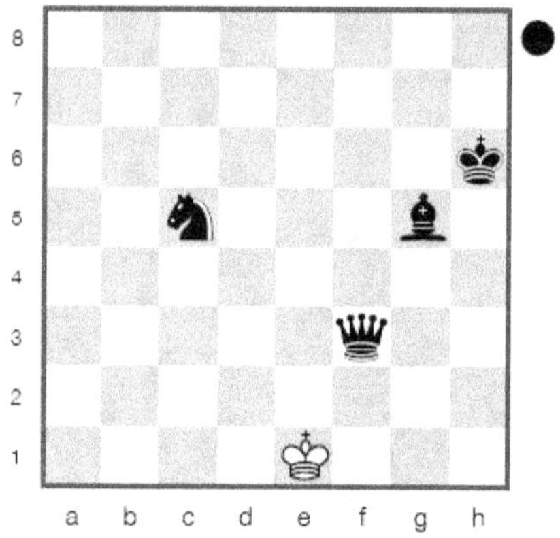

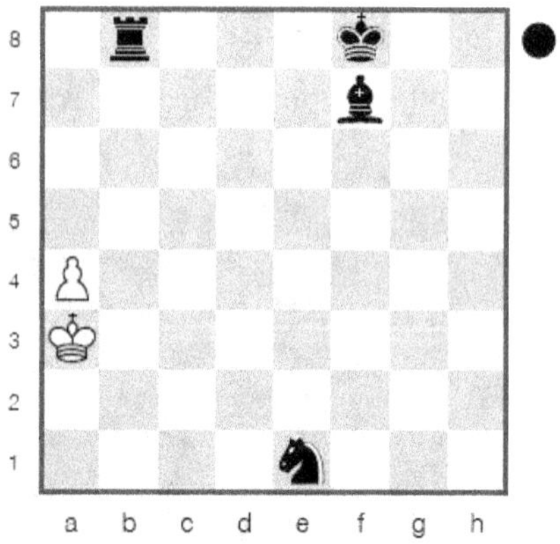

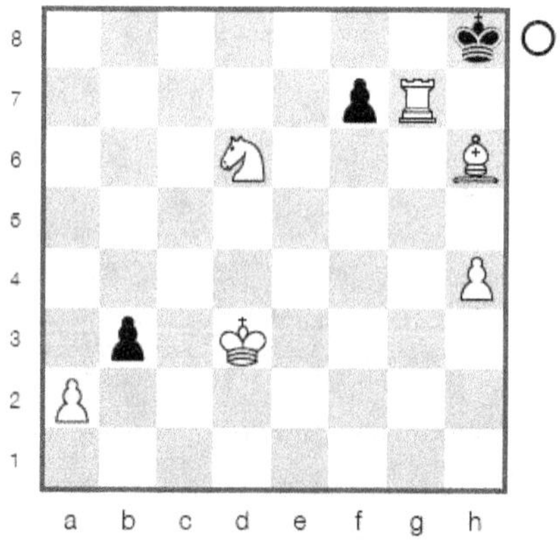

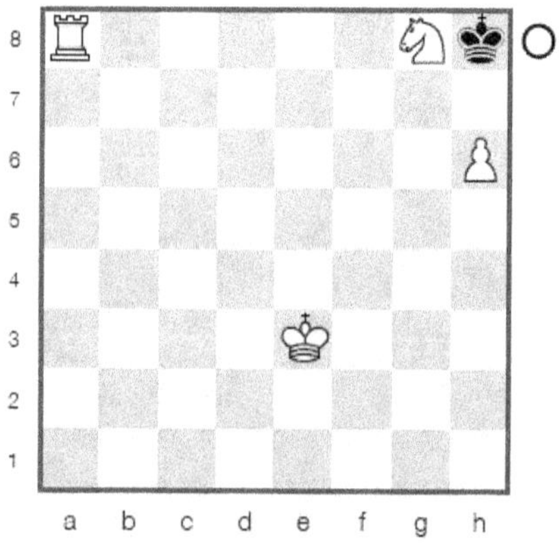

Checkmate with a Pawn

Let's explore how Checkmate can happen with a Pawn, one of your foot soldiers. Pawns typically move forward one square at a time, but they capture diagonally. Let's imagine this scenario: Your Pawn has advanced all the way to your opponent's side of the board and is now in the final rank. When it reaches this far, you can promote it to any other piece, often choosing a Queen for its power. This is a possible scenario leading to Checkmate. However, more scenarios exist here below and I am certain you can find them !

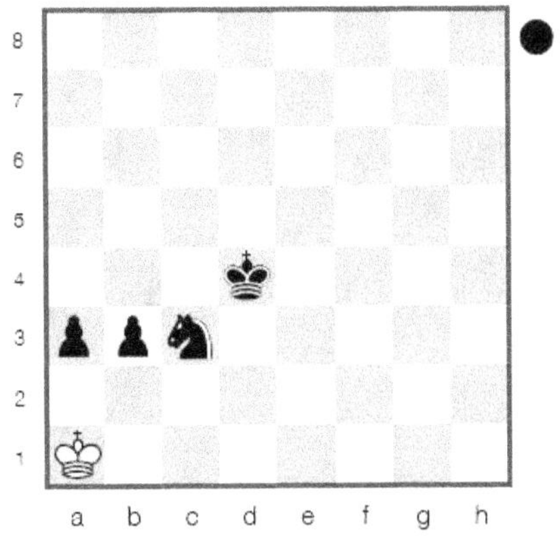

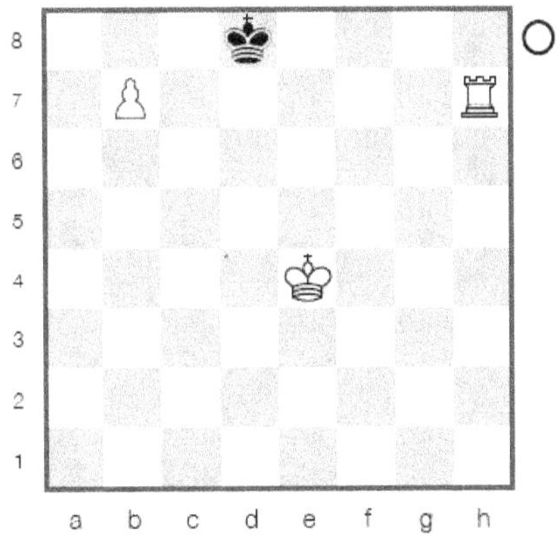

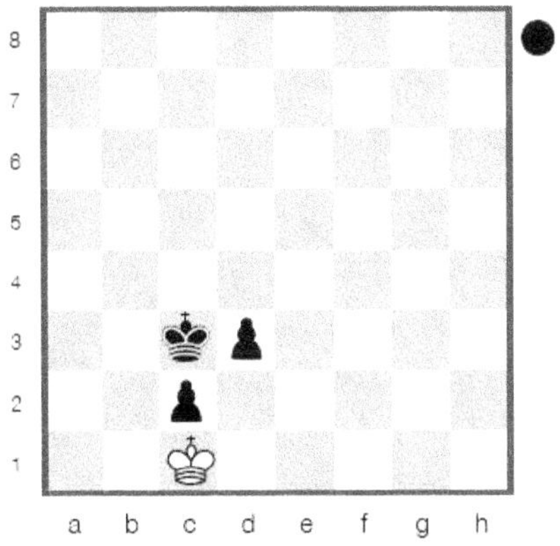

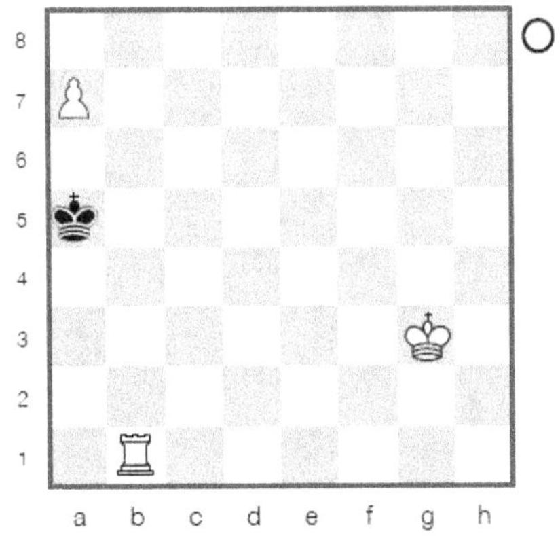

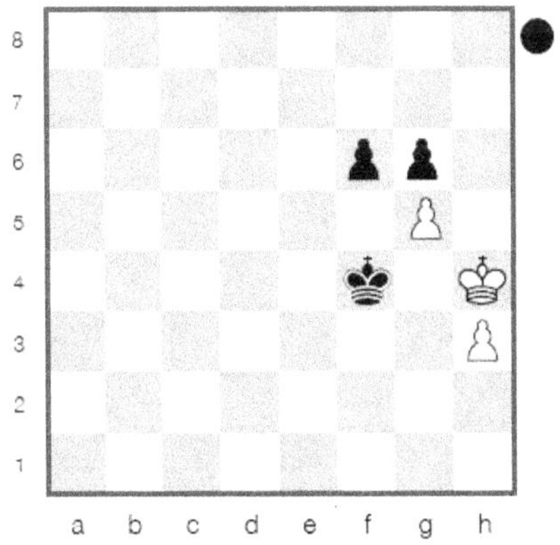

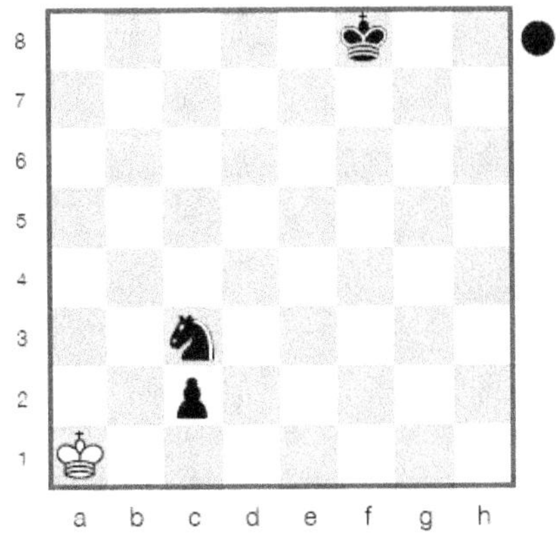

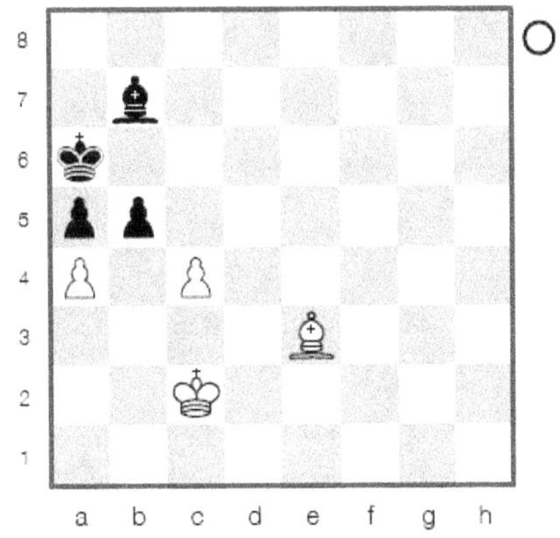

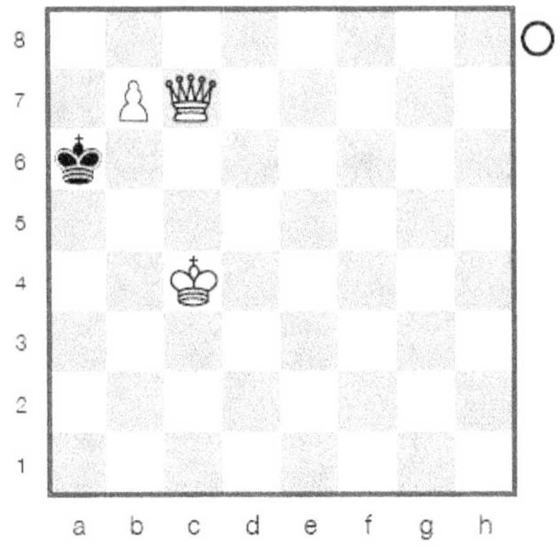

Checkmate with a Queen Puzzles

Think of the Queen as the superhero of chess. In order to make best use of her abilities, It's a good idea to keep your Queen closer to the middle of the chessboard. This way, she can reach the most squares in a single move. The Queen is the piece with the highest number of known Checkmate patterns as she can deliver Checkmate collaborating with any other piece. So, watch carefully at all squares she can reach in one move, some create great occasions. Using your Queen to checkmate is the natural first way to attack the King.

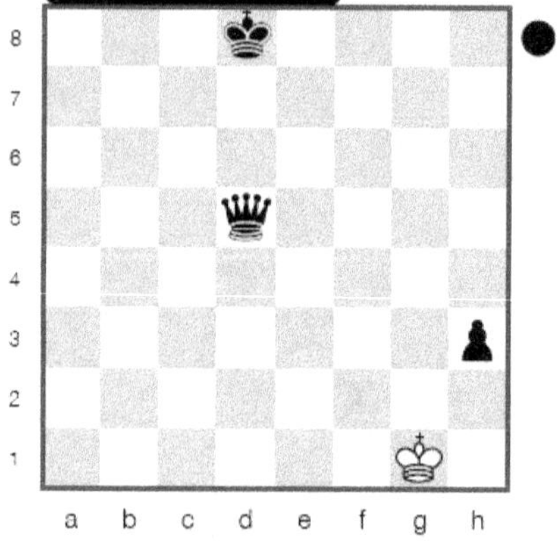

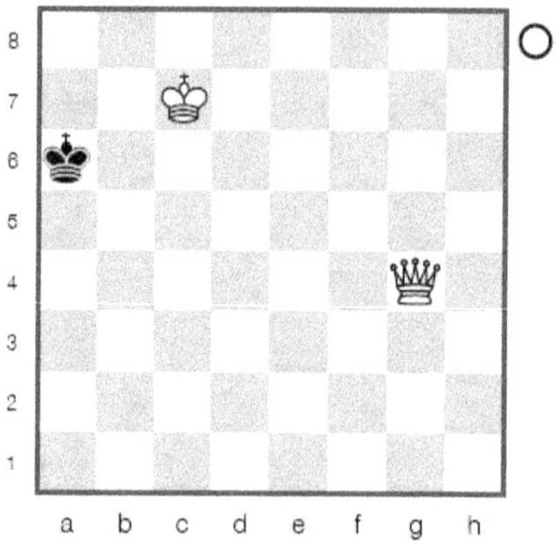

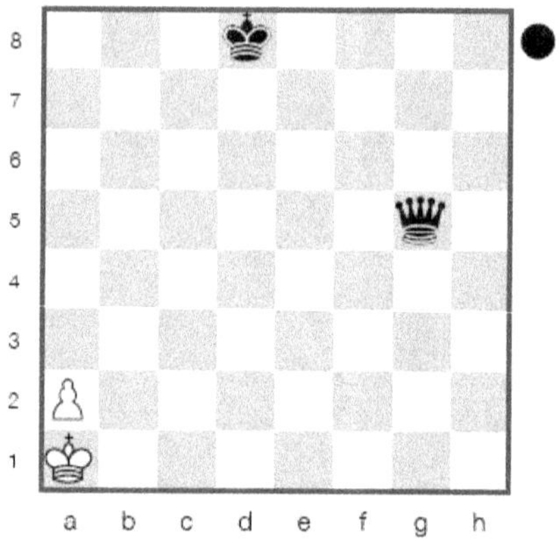

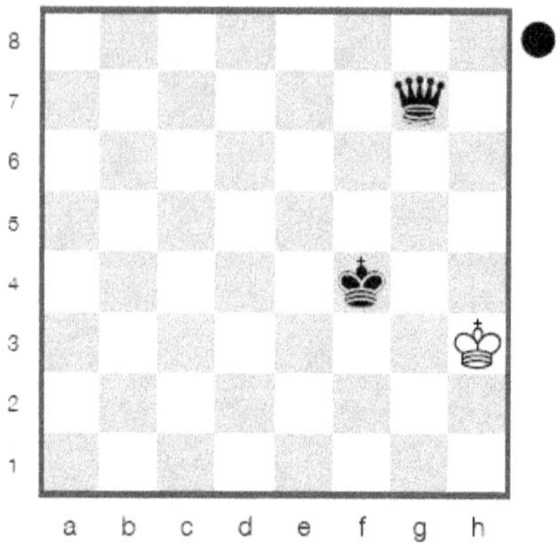

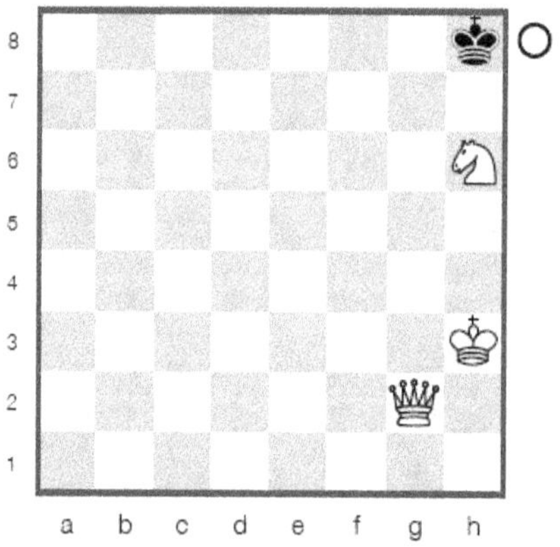

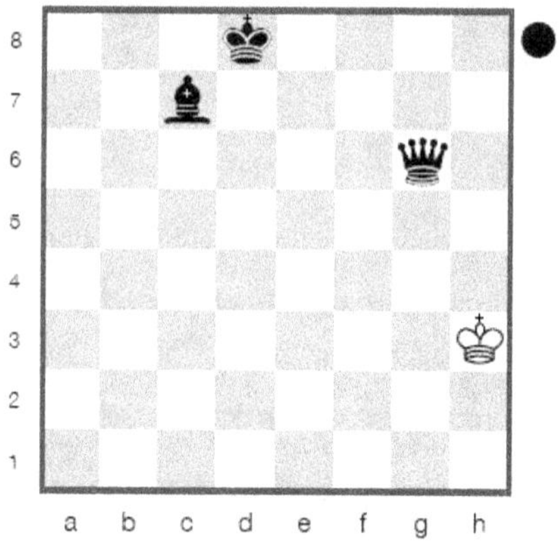

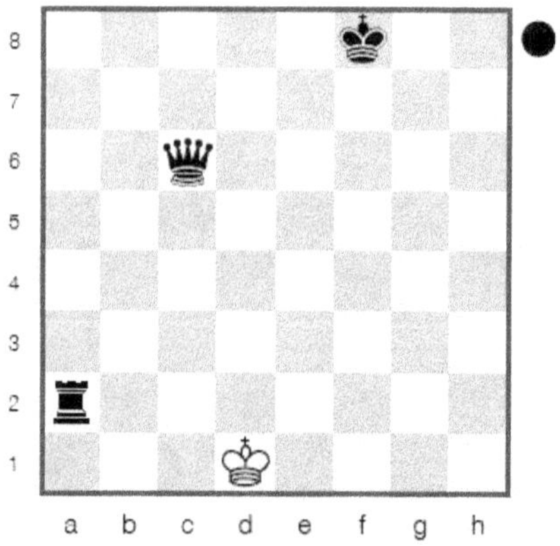

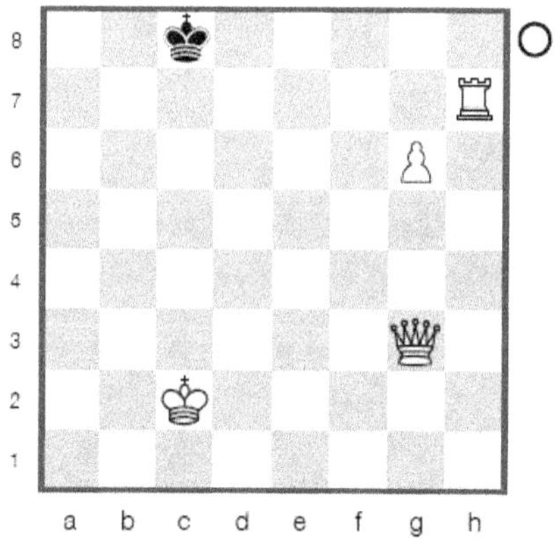

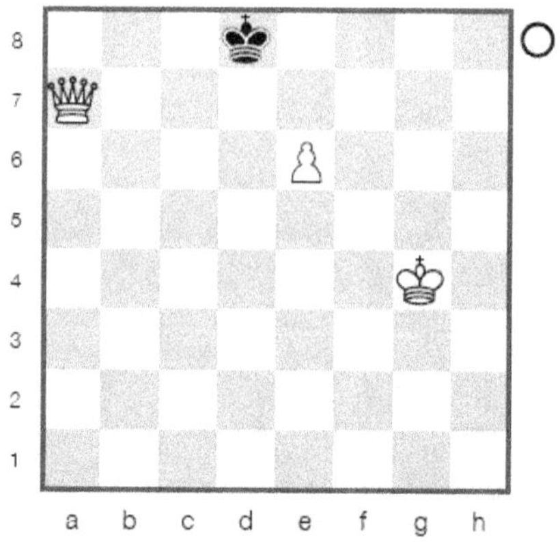

Stalemate

Stalemate is a situation in chess where the player whose turn it is to move is not in check and has no legal move. Stalemate results in a draw. During the endgame, stalemate is a resource that can enable the player with the inferior position to draw the game rather than lose.

Here below are 4 examples of stalemate on the board. Try to understand them !

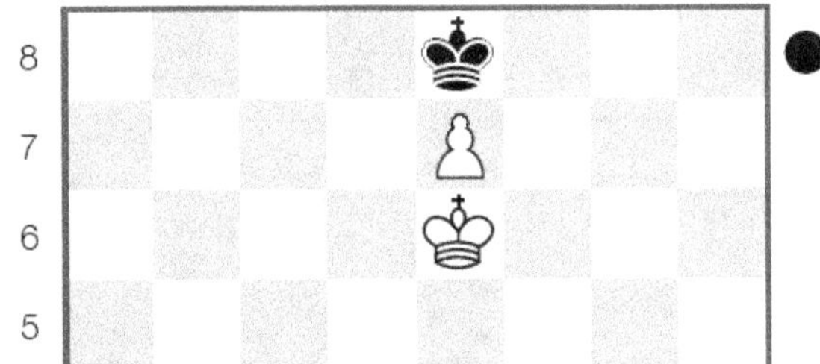

Black to play, only the King remain on e8, safe. d8 and f8 are attacked by the white Pawn. d7, e7 and f7 are adjacent squares to the other King, so inaccessible. The Black King is ssafe but cannot move.
It's Stalemate !

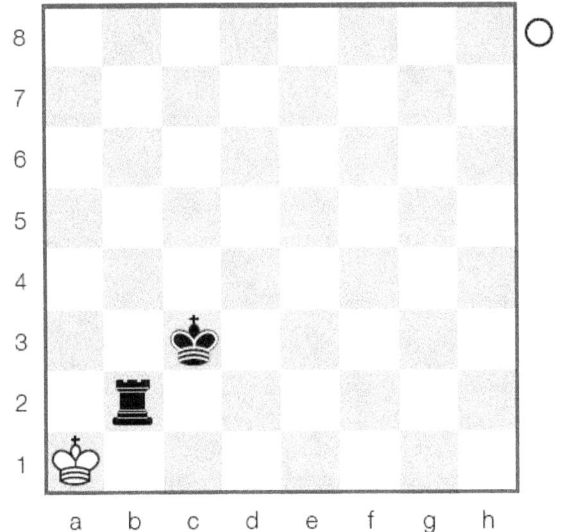

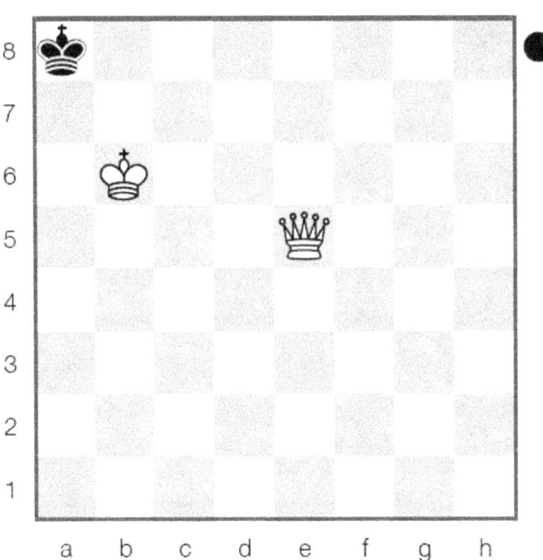

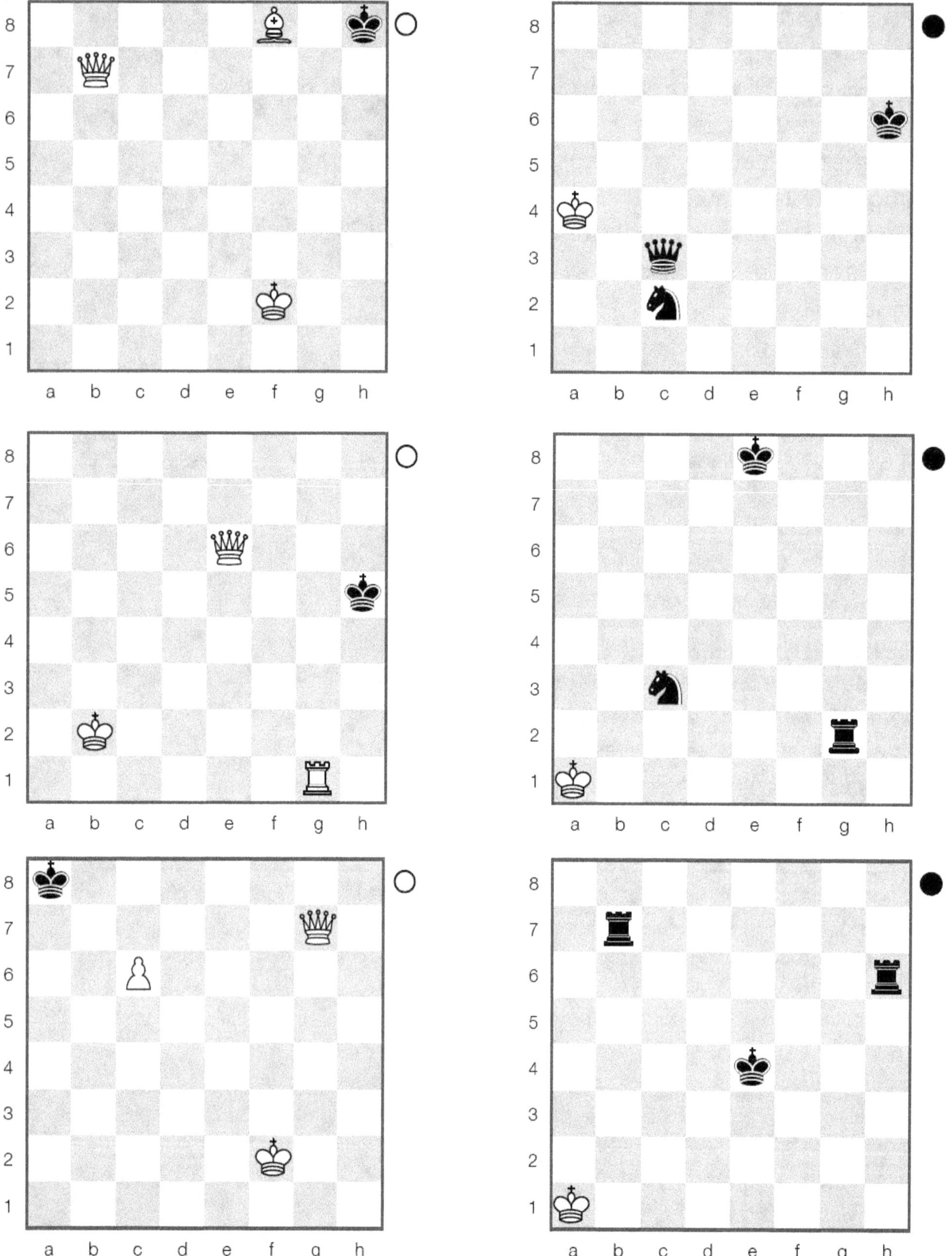

Checkmate in 1 move / B   Puzzles

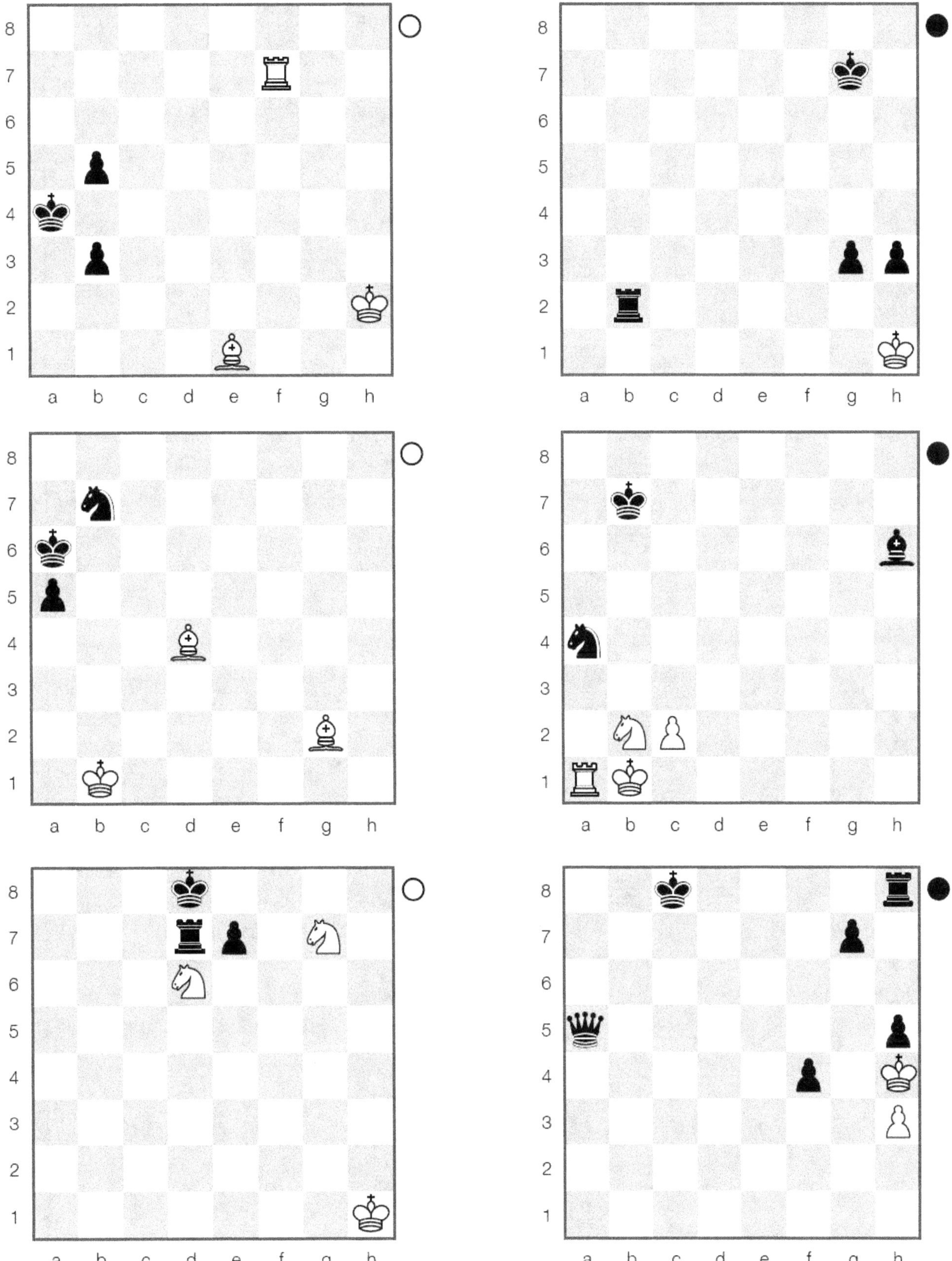

Creating Checkmate   Puzzles

Position the Queen on the board to create a Checkmate

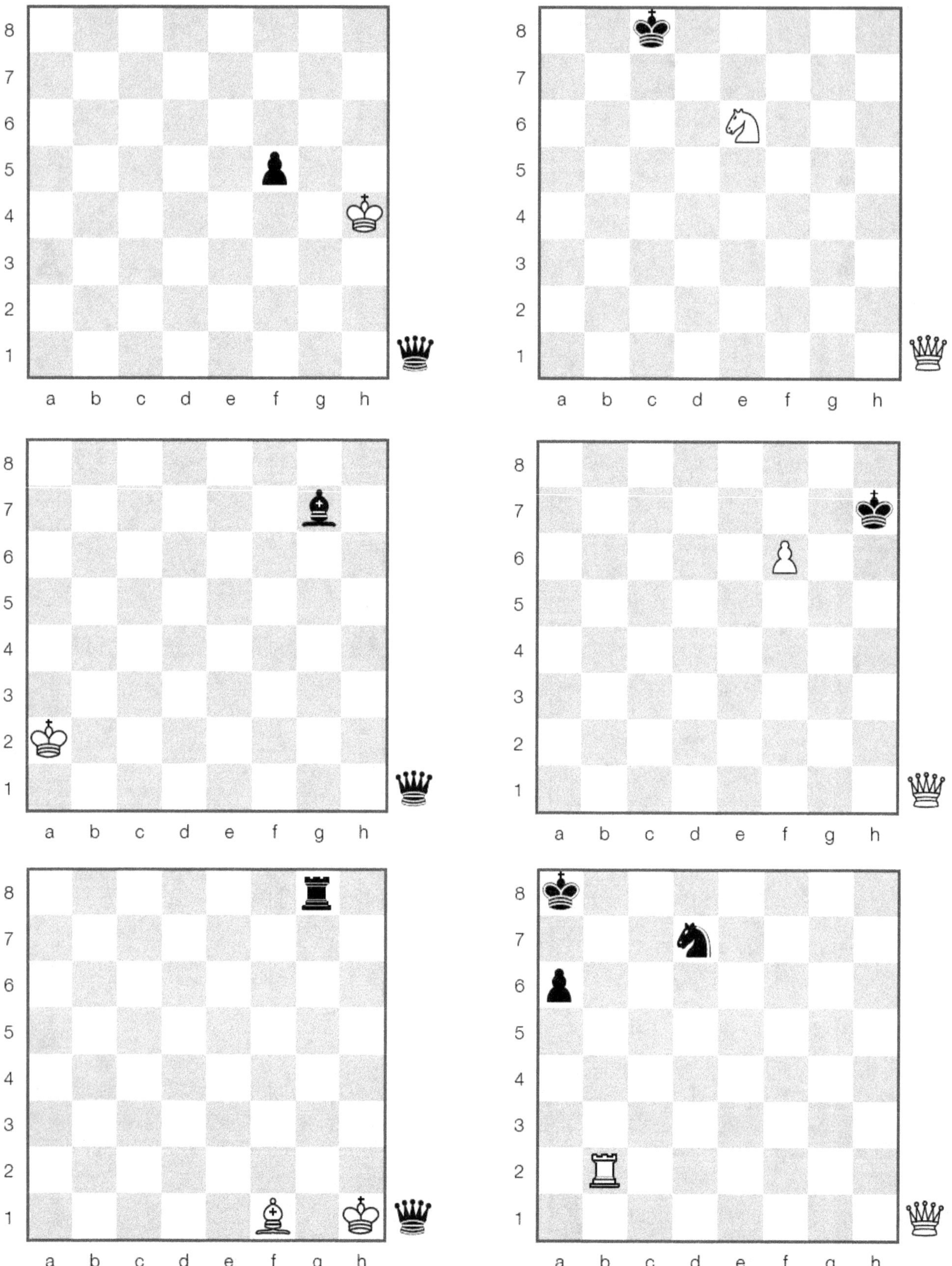

Let's Play Odds Games

In chess, sometimes players are at different skill levels, which can make the game less enjoyable when facing a stronger opponent. To make things fair and fun, we can use 'handicap games', also called 'odds games.
'Odds games are like a balancing act. They help level the playing field when one player is better. We've got six examples of these games for you to try, starting from little balancing change (top left) to the strongest (bottom right). Let's jump in and have a good time!

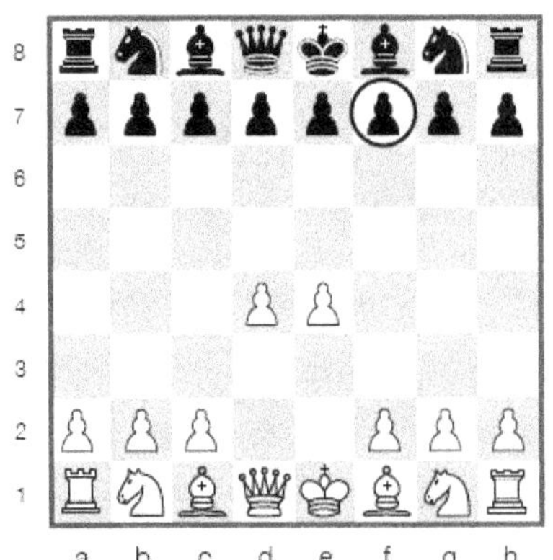

Pawn & 2 moves: the weaker player plays White and start the game playing Pawns twice. Black plays without f7 Pawn.

Knight or Rook: the stronger player Queen's Knight or Queen's Rook is removed.

Two minor pieces: The odds-giver chooses which of their two Knights and/or Bishops to remove

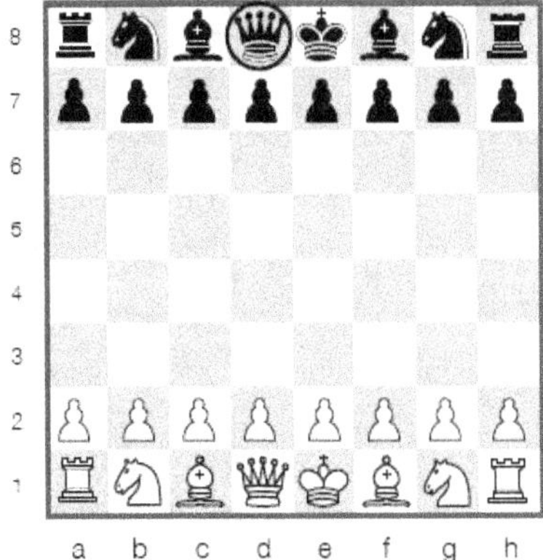

Queen odds: the stronger player's Queen is removed.

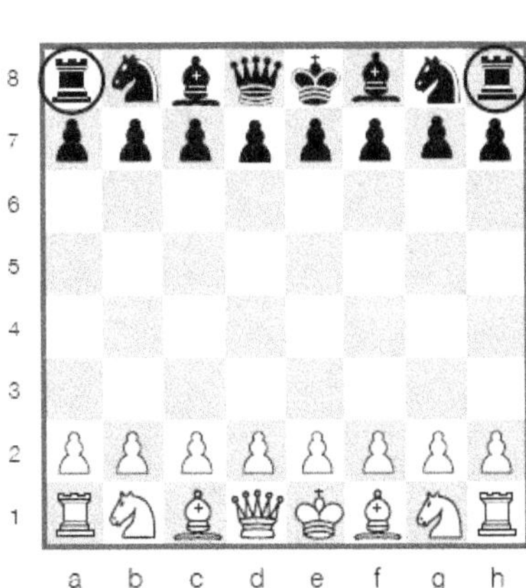

Two rooks: Both Rooks of the stronger player are removed.

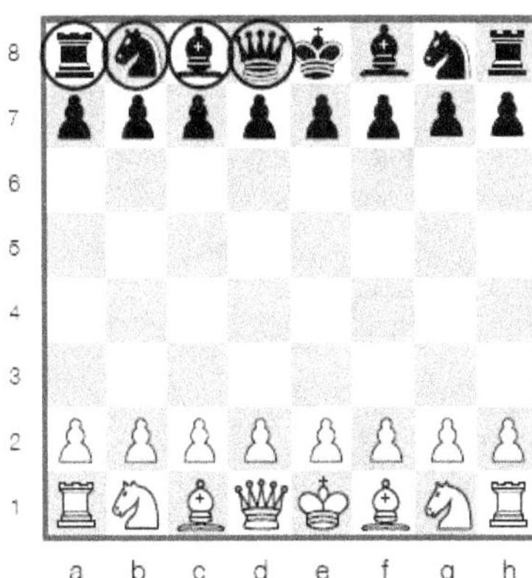

Queenside odds: All queenside pieces, excluding Pawns, of the stronger player are removed.

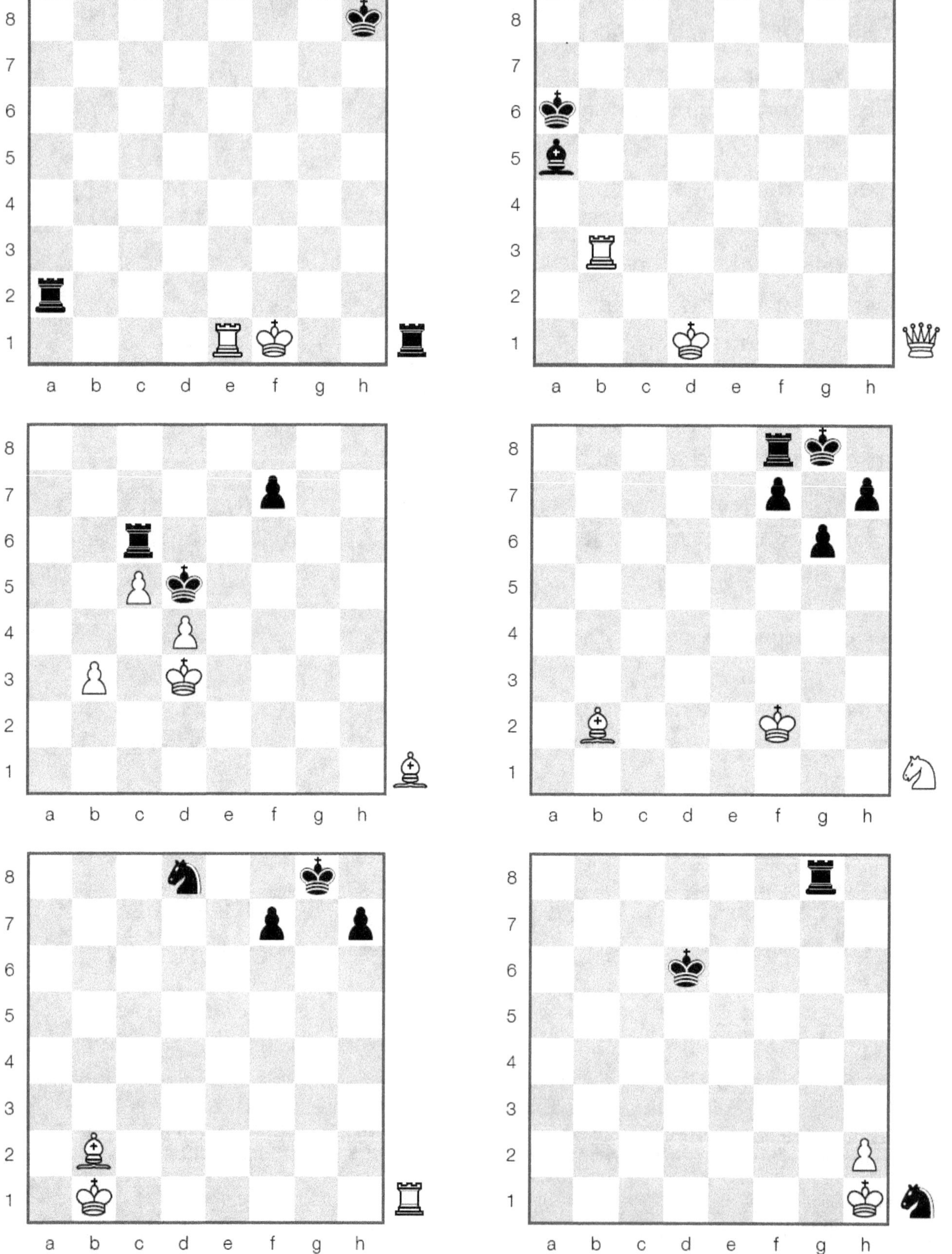

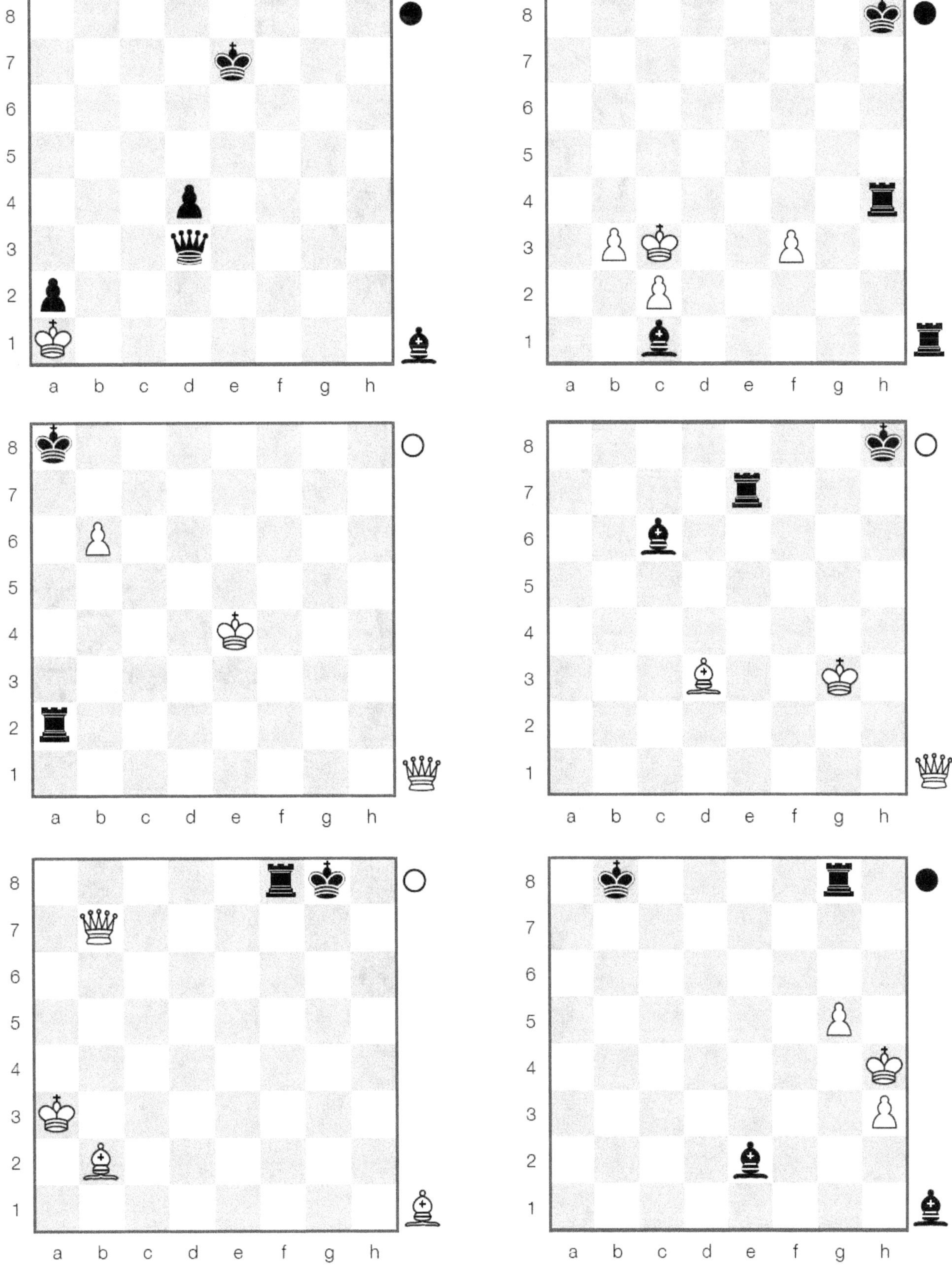

I CAN CHECKMATE

Rules when playing Chess

Pieces movements for example, are formal rules of the game, but informal rules exists as well. They help regulate player's behaviours during a game of Chess.

- You only play with 1 hand and prevent having 2 hands above the board at once.
- You do not let your hand or fingers touching the board or pieces if it is not your turn to play
- Before the first move, and at the end of the game, you shake hands with your opponent.
- We do not make pressure on the other player to play faster. Not verbally and not producing sounds of exasperation.

- We respect in all manners the concentration of the other player.
- 'Touch move' rule: When it is your turn to play, If you touch a piece, you have to play it and not another. If you drop it onto a square, you cannot move it back anymore.
- If you are playing at a tournament and you have any disagreement with the other player, just raise your hand and the referee will come to your table.

Favourable Exchange

We know that chess pieces are not all equal; they have distinct appearances and names because they move differently. Some pieces can cover many squares in one move, while others have a more limited range. Let's compare a Bishop to a Queen: in one move, the Bishop can reach 13 squares, whereas the Queen can move to 27 squares!

So, it's natural that we prefer a Bishop over a Pawn or a Queen over a Rook. To help us understand their relative values, we assign them their equivalence in number of Pawns:

Knight	---	3 Pawns
Bishop	---	3 Pawns
Rook	-----	5 Pawns
Queen	---	9 Pawns

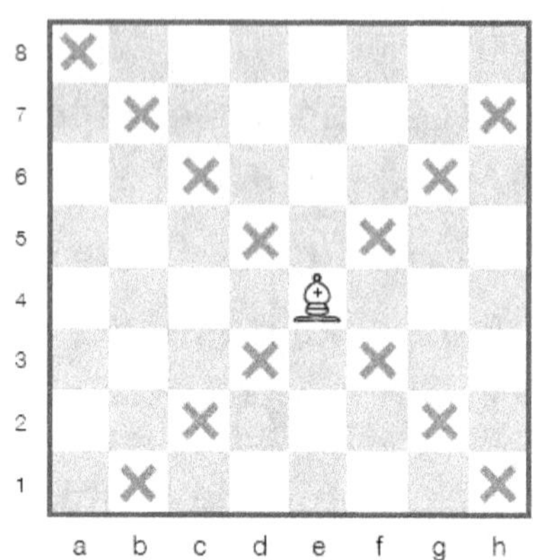

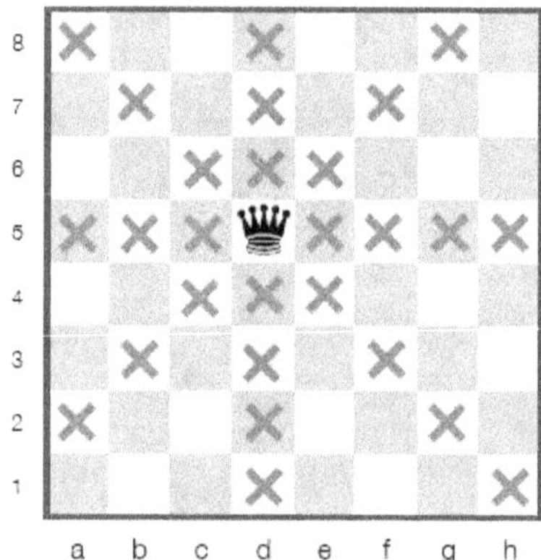

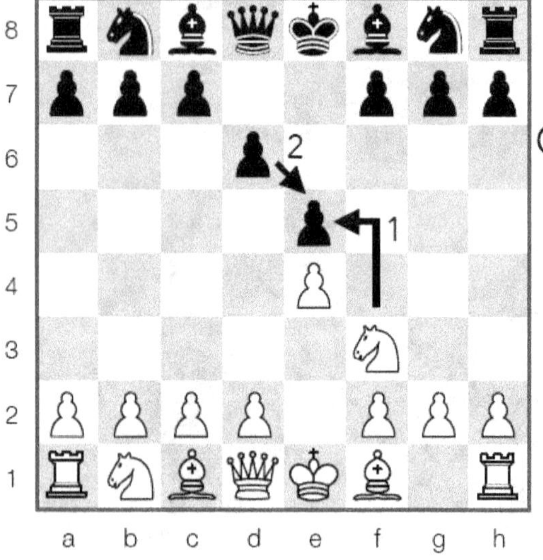

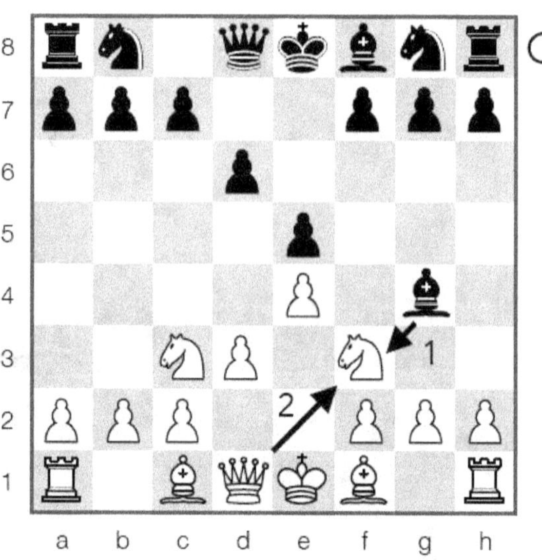

You are playing as White. If you capture the black Pawn with your Knight (1), you will lose your Knight (2) in return. In other words; you gain a Pawn but lose a Knight. From White perspective, this exchange is <u>unfavorable</u>. However, for Black, it is a <u>favorable</u> exchange

You play as White. If the black Bishop captures your Knight (1), you can capture the Bishop with your Queen (2).
It is an <u>equal exchange</u>.

Favourable Exchange

Practice

Find the best Exchange in your favour

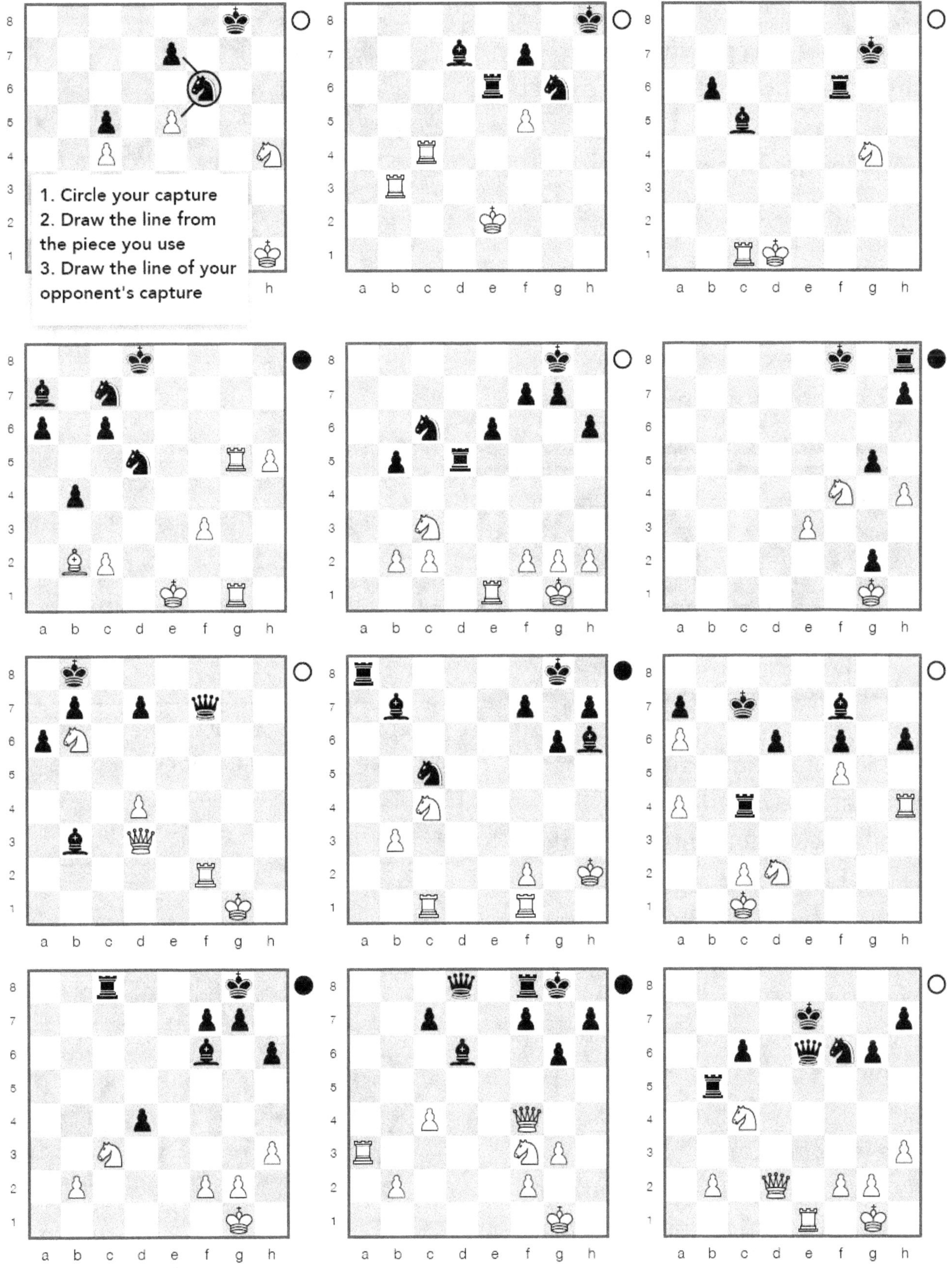

Time Control & Chess Clocks

Way back when your grandfather's grandfather was playing Chess, sometimes those chess games lasted more than a day.

So, we've got to have chess clocks to make sure that the Chess game cannot last forever.

Chess Clocks are useed to determine a certain amount of time, either for the entire game or for a block of moves. These clocks allow

as well to have incremental time added after every move. So, you definitely cacn find the format that please you and your pbest Chess performing style the most. If you're playing in a tournament you might have for example, 30 minutes for each player, for the entire game, meaning it can last one hour. If you run out of time on your clock before there is a checkmate, you generally lose the game. When you play with a Chess clock, you should use the same hand to play the piece and tap the clock.

When you start playing online   with friends or other players you do not know, you commonly have the option to play bullet, blitz, rapid or classical games, but you definitely should give it a try to each of them, you only could find more fun !

Bullet Game: 1-3 minutes for each player
Blitz Game: 5 minutes for each player
Rapid Game: 10-15 minutes for each player
Classic Game: up to 7 hours

Best Ways to Use your Rooks

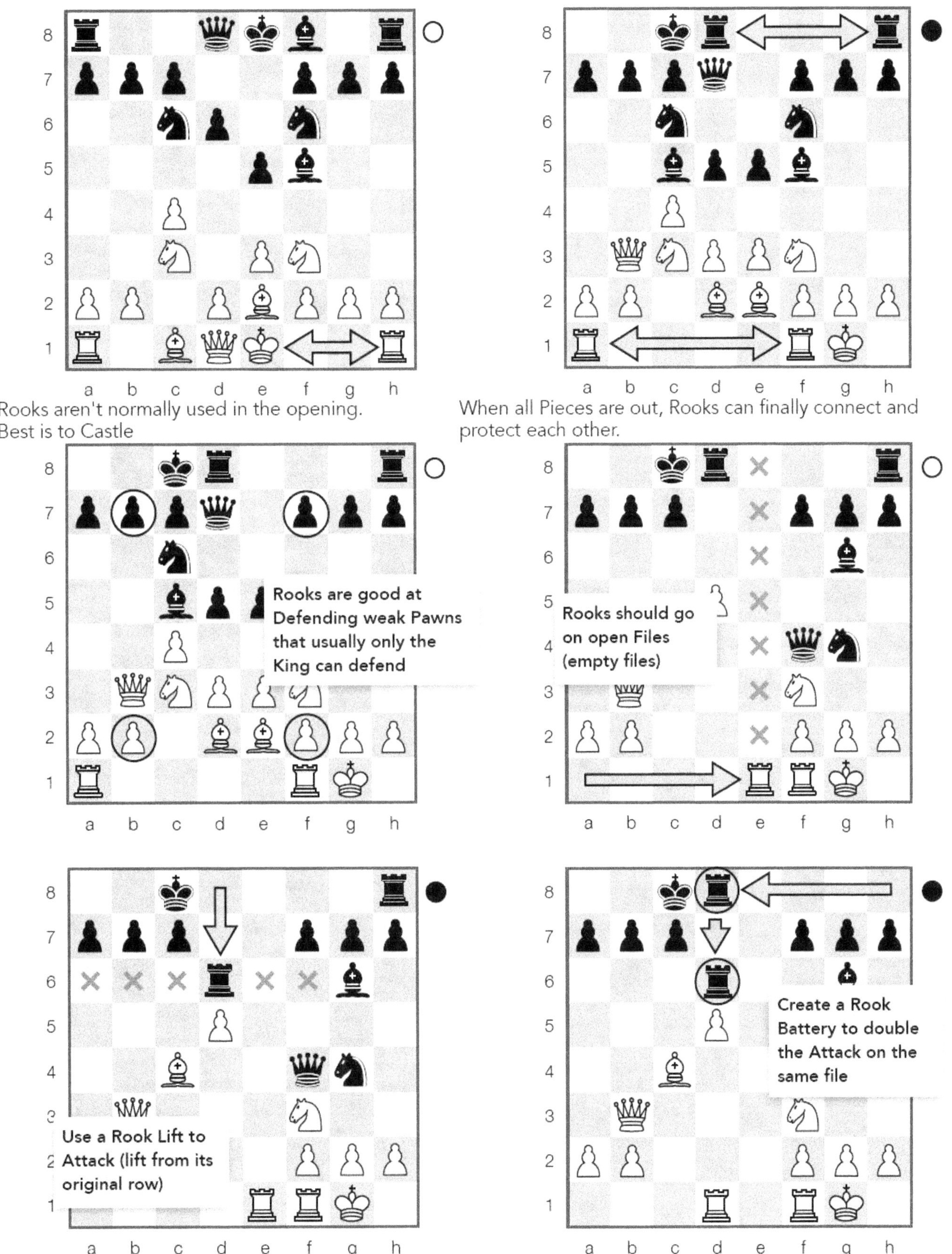

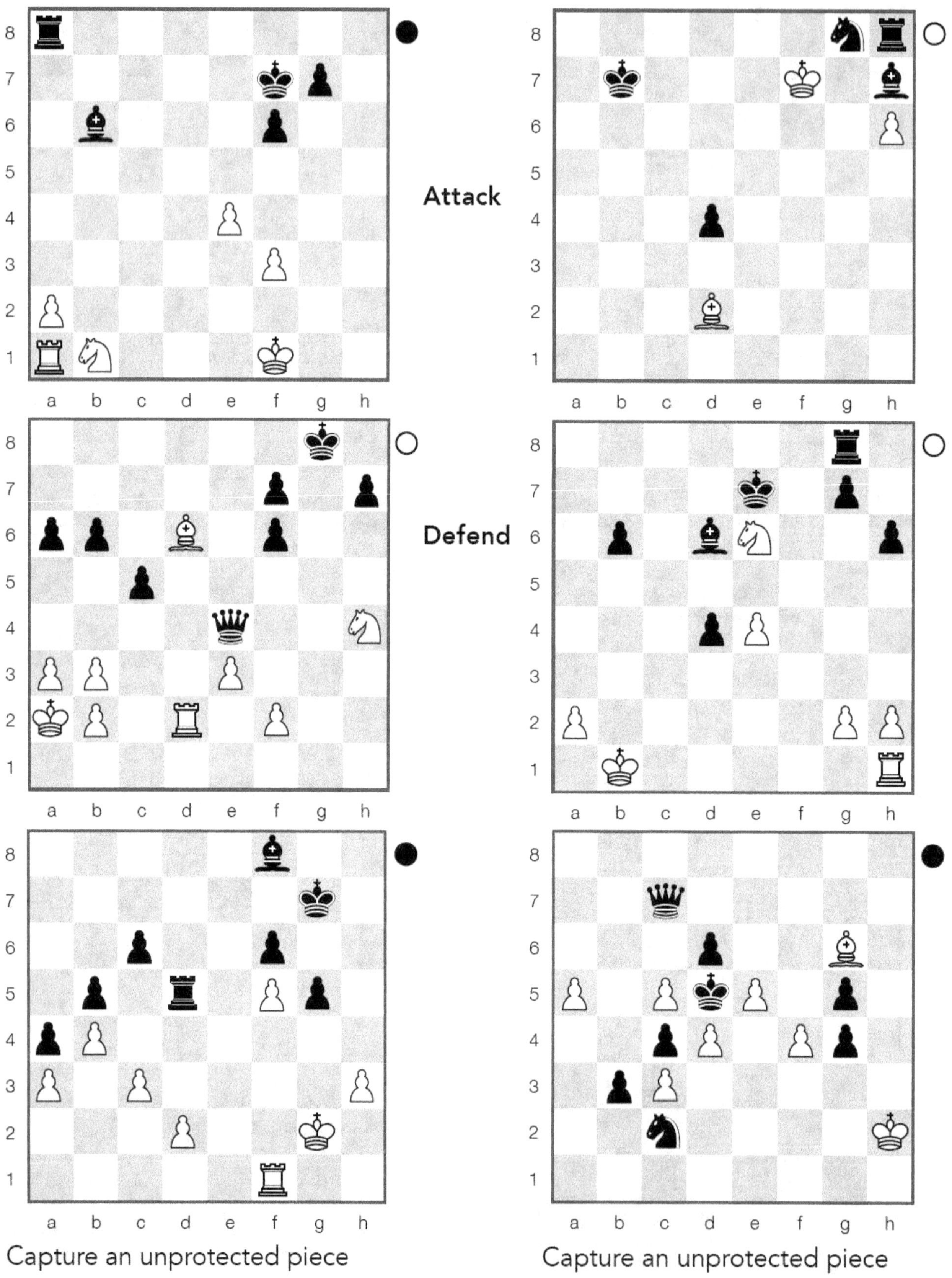

Attack

Defend

Capture an unprotected piece   Capture an unprotected piece

Best Ways to Use Bishops & Knights

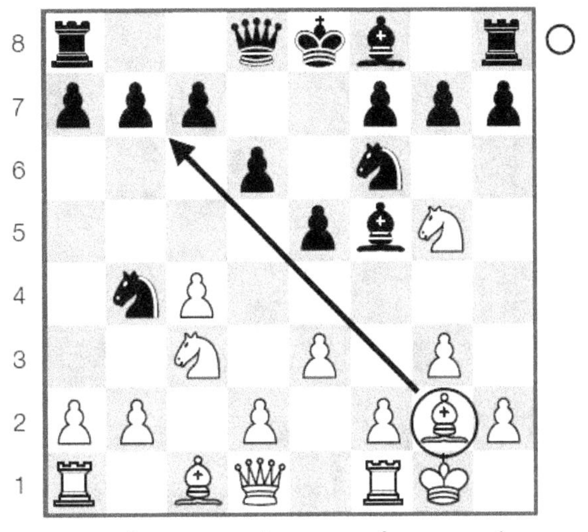

Bishops are usually best placed on long diagonals in order to control more squares

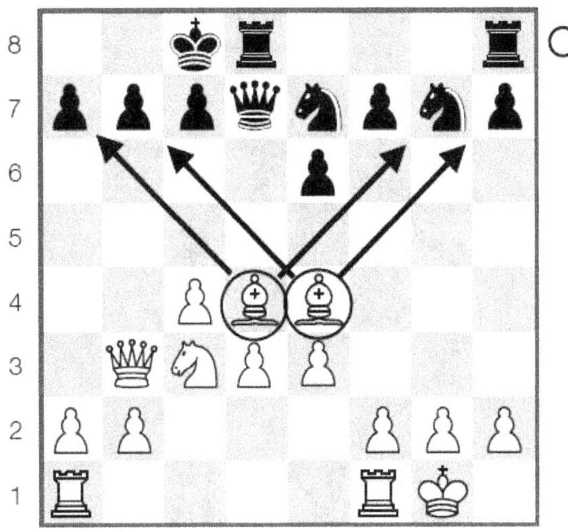

Bishops work very well side by side as they cover both colors of the board.

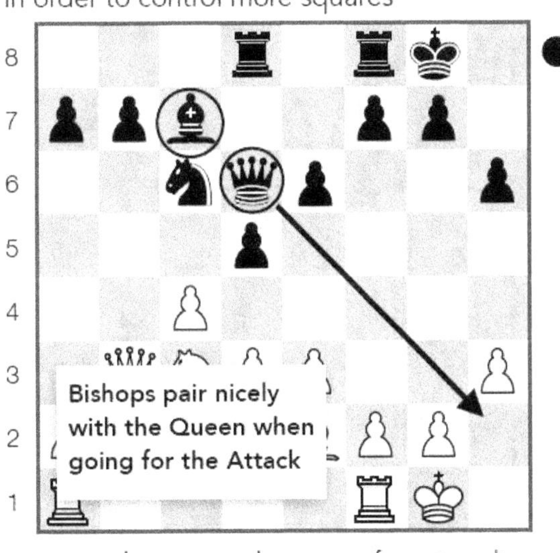

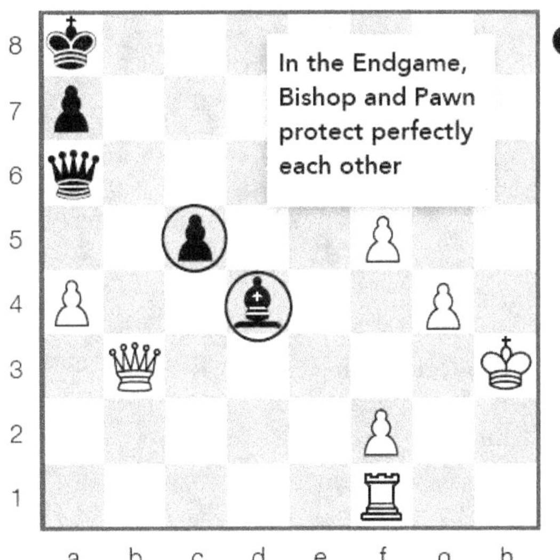

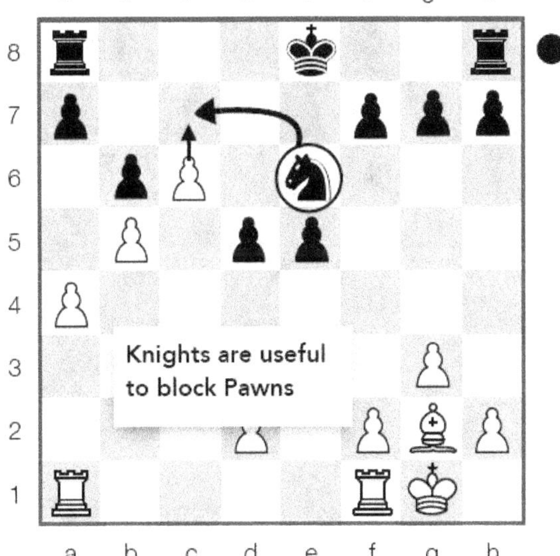

Best Ways to Use Queen & Pawns

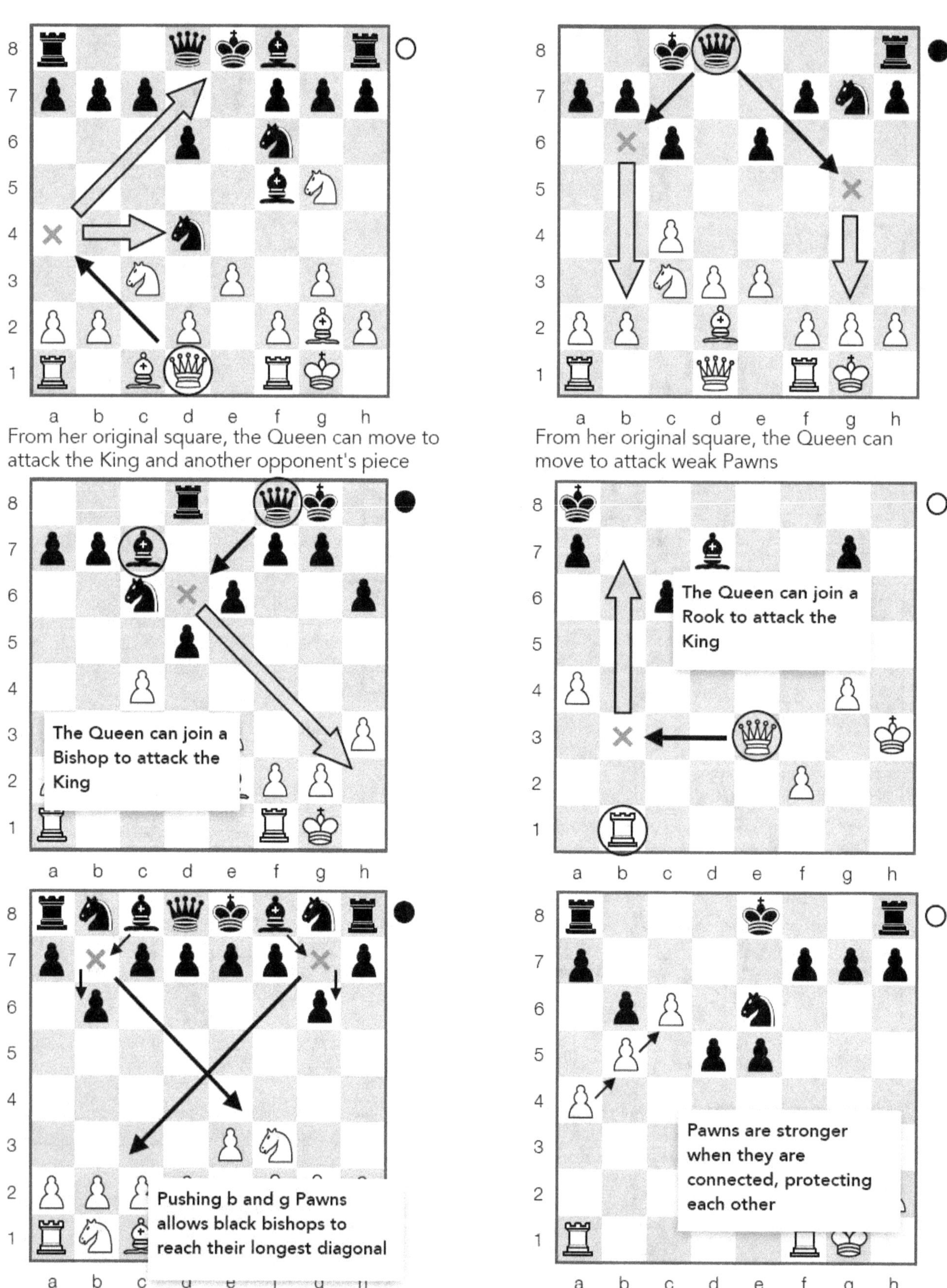

From her original square, the Queen can move to attack the King and another opponent's piece

From her original square, the Queen can move to attack weak Pawns

Chess Notation

Chess Notation is used to record moves made in a game of Chess. Around the world, players participating to offline Chess tournaments are asked to annotate their games to have them officially recorded. For a young student, Chess notation is first of all a fun way to materialize the experience of decision making. Later on, it become a tool to write down its own games and review then, as well as reading and learning from expectional games of the past. Kids got very excited when a running clock hurry them to synchronize thinking, playing and writing.

The most important symbols are:
'+' is used to indicate the King is Check
'#' means there is Checkmate
'd8=Q' means a Pawn on d8 is promoted into a Queen
'0-0' for King side Castling
'0-0-0' for Queen side Castling

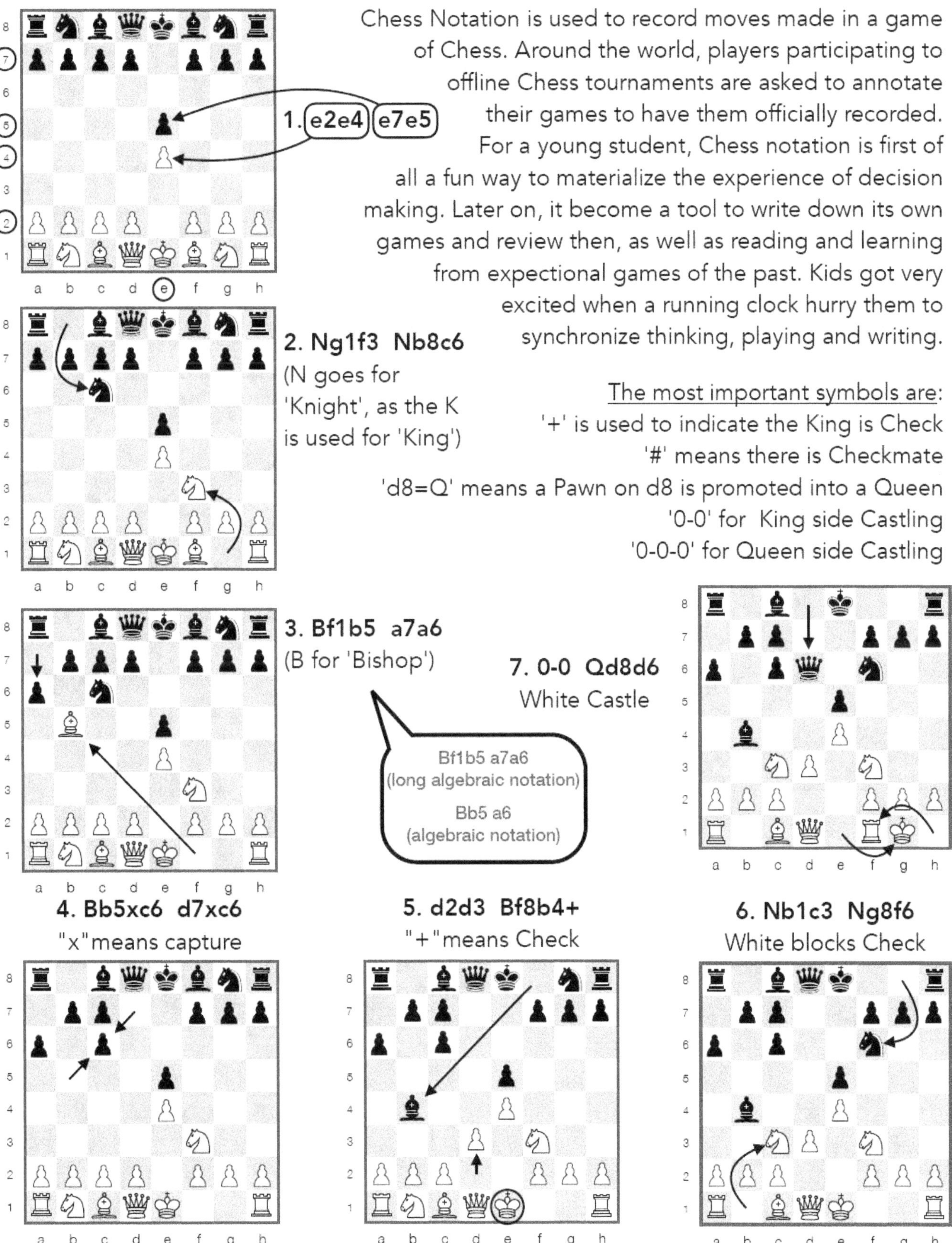

Chess Ladder Final Test   A

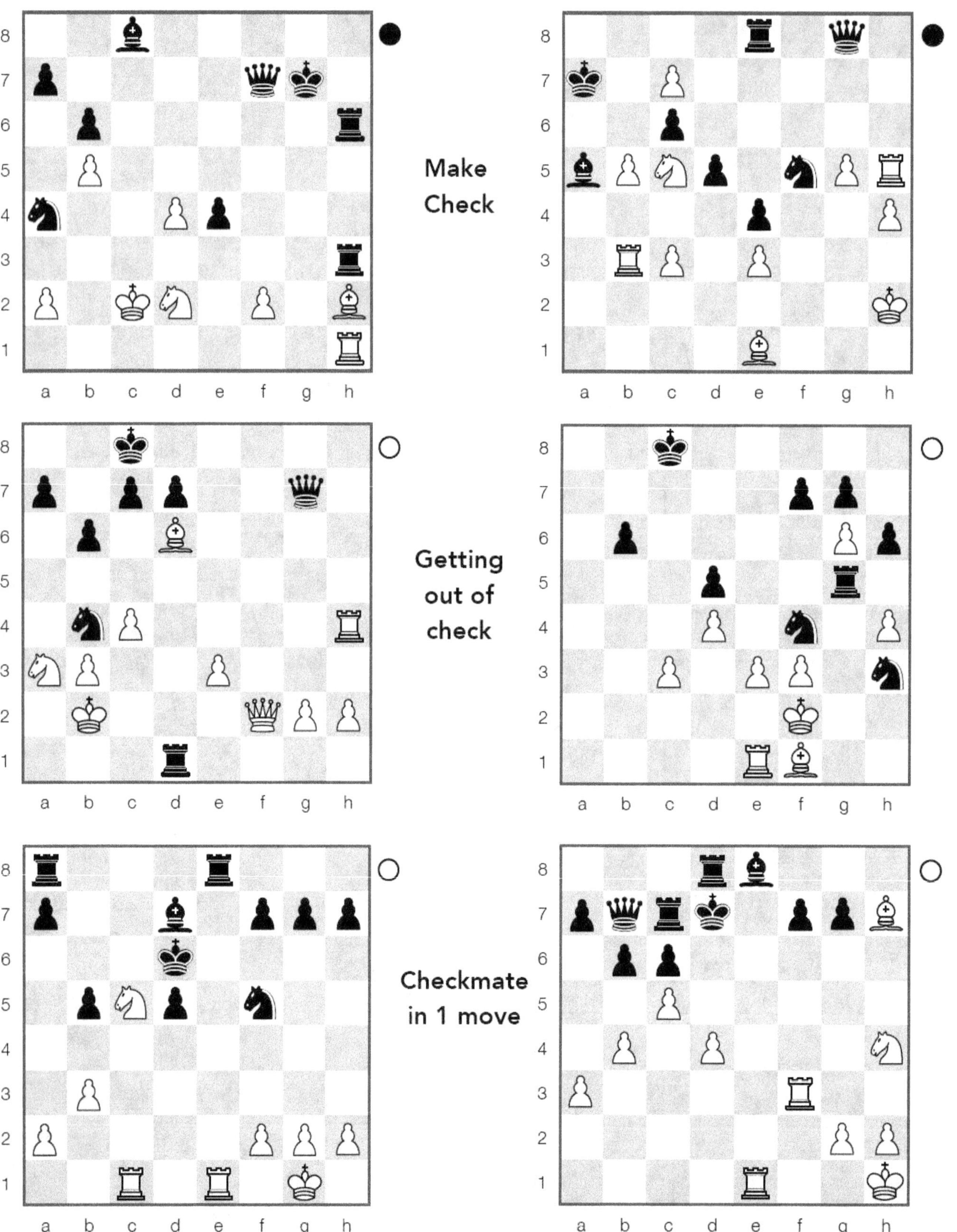

Chess Ladder Final TestB

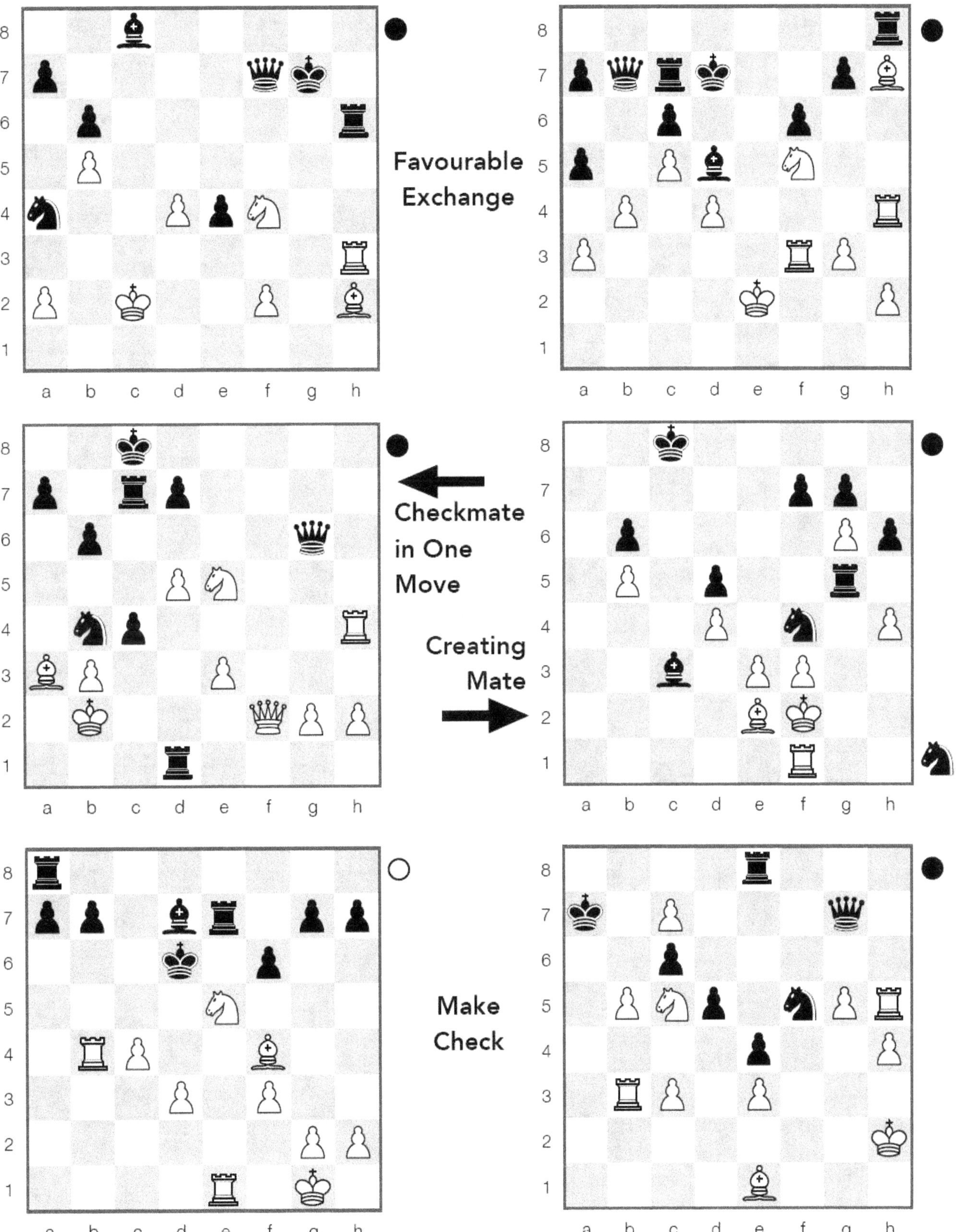

Chess Game Scorecard

#	WHITE	BLACK	#	WHITE	BLACK
1			31		
2			32		
3			33		
4			34		
5			35		
6			36		
7			37		
8			38		
9			39		
10			40		
11			41		
12			42		
13			43		
14			44		
15			45		
16			46		
17			47		
18			48		
19			49		
20			50		
21			51		
22			52		
23			53		
24			54		
25			55		
26			56		
27			57		
28			58		
29			59		
30			60		

SIGNATURE

SIGNATURE

I AM A CHESS PLAYER

Organizing a Class Tournament

Class Tournaments are essentials to bring the thrill of being challenged; of taking the risk to lose, to be a better thinker, to know better... I like to say that Chess has this particularity to challenge us with ourselves.

Chess tournaments are also necessary. They bring fun and excitement after the dose of theory. Competition is also appreciated by kids and it serves the greater purpose of pulling kids up.

A Class of Chess usually lasts 60 or 90 min. In both cases, it is the number of sessions and students that will determine the type of tournament you want to implement. Let's see below, for a class of 8 students, what are the options of formats we could use.

<u>Round-Robin</u>: In this tournament format, each participant plays every other participant 1 time. A win awards 1 point, a loss is 0 point, and a tie awards 1/2 point to each player. The player with the highest total score wins the tournament. Assuming that every student plays a match at every class-day, 8 classes-days would be needed (7 classes-days of tournament + 1 class-day for the results and awards distribution). Free online tools will help you create match schedules. These tools ensure that players don't face each other repeatedly and that everyone gets a fair number of games with both White and Black pieces.

Round-Robin Class Tournament (8 students / 8 classes days)

	John	Mary	Mark	Denis	Tony	Chris	Karen	Anne
John								
Mary								
Mark								
Denis								
Tony								
Chris								
Karen								
Anne								

<u>Swiss System</u>: The Swiss system tournament comes as a solution when the number of classes is too limited to implement a Round-Robin format.

Swiss System Class Tournament (8 students / 3 classes-days)

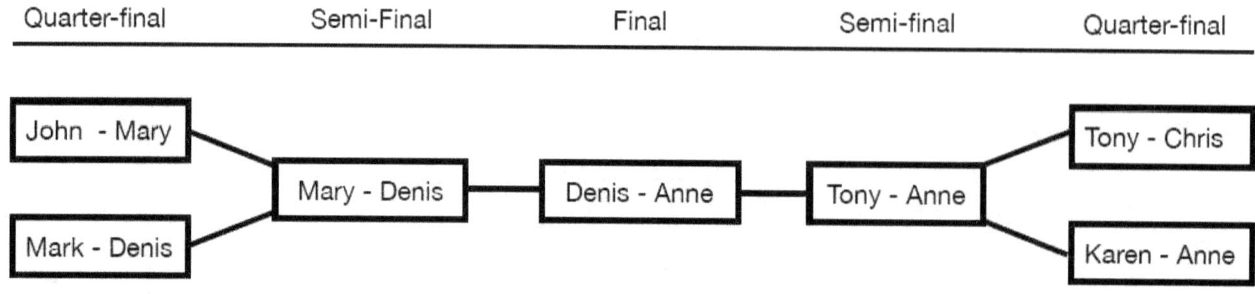

Benefits of playing Chess

Beside the pleasure playing Chess provides to people of all ages for centuries, its benefits in socializing, building personality and revealing character, Chess is mostly known for its positive impact on Cognitions.
In the left picture, the 3 lower levels of thinking skills, 'Remember', 'Understand' & 'Apply', are the basis of most educational systems. However, thinking skills from above, 'Analyze', 'Evaluate' & 'Create', are rarely developped. These 3 stages of higher thinking skills are actually composed of critical thinking and creative thinking. Chess is an ideal activity to stimulate these higher skills.

CRITICAL THINKING	CREATIVE THINKING	MORE STIMULATIONS
Logical Thinking and Reasoning	Create something new or Original	Concentration
Comparing	Flexibility	Attention
Classifying	Originality	Space management
Planning & Sequencing	Fluidity	Acceptance of Contrarian Ideas
Cause and Effect	To Elaborate	Control of reflex actions
Modeling	Brainstorming	Jugement
Analogies	To Modify	Thinking before acting
Deductive & Inductive Reasoning	Imagining	Decision Making
Building an Hypothesis	To Associate	Taking responsibility for decisions made
Criticizing	Listing Attributes	Ethical sense, general behavior.
Knowing, Manage and Understand better ourselves and our environment. Better orient ourselves and make our choices.	Metaphorical Thinking	Positive impact on Literacy, Science, Technology and Mathematics

Sometimes we don't know what to play

It is my turn to play, here are the questions I should make...
- Can I make checkmate? Not yet probably, but if you see you can make Check in 1 move, then you should very probably spend some time looking at which square is the least protected and bring another attacker to it.
- What did the other player moved. What does it change on the board?
- so, first thing to look at is to make sure all of my pieces are protected
- If some piece is attacked, I have to protect it, but wait, maybe I can capture some bigger piece ;)
- Ok, no big piece to capture & no piece of mine is attacked, what to do? I should look wether I can capture any piece that my opponent does not protect.
- Capture is good but sometimes It's better to develop my pieces. Look at the next page to understand what means to develop your pieces.
- ...and by the way, meanwhile the other player is thinking, I can also think.

Course Advices for Teachers and Coaches

- Each Class Day should have a single clear topic, composed of a variety of ways to understand it
- For each individual Kid, measure the progress, and take individual action with 1 on 1 adjustment. Meanwhile, let the other kids play.
- Organise a class tournament as soon as all kids are able to move the pieces and understand capture, defense, Check and getting out of Check. Checkmate abilities will take more time and there is no need to wait for it.
- Kids will insist to play with their best friend, but Players rotation is beneficial; everyone plays with everyone, it is part of the inter-personal experience Chess provides.
- Respecting the rule's game is how conflicts are prevented (one hand on the board, and only when it is my turn to play. Let the other player take time to think, within reasonable limits. Touch move rules applied.
- Teach Kids how to play online anytime they want to.
- There will always be better students than others, and that happens with Chess too. Some will brag about it and try to intimidate the weaker players. Do not let it happen. Ask the good player to tell the class how he found good moves, as well as you could ask the weaker player to explain what he missed. Mistakes are not to be hidden, but instead they should be exposed and systematically used as a source of energy to improve our performance on the board - a concept applicable to everything in life.

Solutions to Puzzles

Solutions that can be provided by an assisting adult:
p9, The Chess Board
p10, The Right Square
p11, Chicken on the Board!
p12, Chicken on the Board 2
p13, Board Orientation
p19, Pieces Reach
p23, Count to Move
P24, Pieces Reach 2

The Following answers are partially written in Algebraic Notation, which is a shorter (and more common) version of the 'Long Algebraic Notation' explained on page 77.

Order of Answers

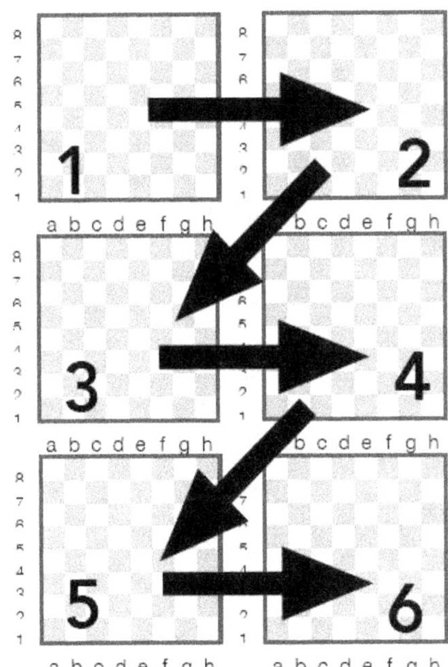

p29, Move & Take Pieces:
(In these Puzzless, we do not expect yet the student to see 'unsafe squares')
1. Example
2. Circle a5, d8 / cross d6
3. Circle c5, d8 / cross a5, d6
4. Circle b2, g3 / cross c3, d4, f4, d6, c7, b8
5. Circle c7 / cross b4, c5, c6, d4
6. Circle b3, e5, g2 / cross c4, c5, d-4, d6-8, e4, e6, f3
7. Circle b6 / cross b5, b7, c5, d6
8. Circle e3, g3 / cross f3, f4
9. Circle d5, f5 / cross c2, d1, f1, g4

p30, Move & Take Pieces 2:
1. Rg4:Circle d4, g6 / cross c4-f4, g1-g3, g5, h4
2. Qe3: Circle e6, g5 / cross b3-h3, e1-e5, c1, d2, f4, g1, f2, d4, c5, b6, a7
3. Ng4: Circle f6, h6 / cross e5, e3, f2, h2
4. Qc5: Circle a5, d5, f8 / cross a3, a7, b4-b6, c6-c8, d6, e7, d4, e3, f2, g1
5. Bf5: Circle d7, e4 / cross e6, g4, h3, g6, h7
6. f4: Circle g3 / cross f3
7. Qd3: Circle d2, e2, g6 / cross 3rd rank, d4-d8, b1, c2, e4, f5, c4, b5, a6.
8. Nh1: Cross g3
9. Bc6: Circle a4, g2 / cross b5, d7, a8, b7, d5, e4, f3

p32, Hanging Piece:
1. Example
2. QxR
3. NxR
4. QxNf8
5. QxR
6. f4xN
7. Qxd2
8. g2xB
9. QxB

p33, Hanging Piece 2:
1. Nxe5
2. RxB
3. Kxg2
4. NxR
5. d2xB
6. NxB
7. Qxa5
8. NxRa6
9. RxB
10.QxR
11.Bxc7
12.c6xN

P36, Attacking:
1. Example
2. Rd3
3. Kg2
4. Be3
5. e3 e4
6. d5 d4
7. e4e5
8. Ne4
9. Qe3
10.Qf3
11.Bf8
12.Rf2

p37, Attacking
1. Example
2. Example
3. Kg2
4. Bb8
5. d2d4
6. Rf6
7. Nf5
8. g5g4
9. Qd6
10.Qc2
11.Bg1
12.f3 f4

p38, Attacking the King
1. Be5+
2. Nf8+
3. Rg7+
4. h7h5+
5. Qf5+
6. Rh2+

p40, Creating an Attack
1. Nf1
2. Bh2
3. Kb7
4. Queen f6-8, g5 or h5
5. Re1
6. Nf7

p41, Attacking
1. f5f6
2. Bd1
3. f5f6
4. d5d4
5. Bd6
6. Rd6
7. Qh5

8. Bf8
9. Kb5
10.Qc7
11.Ne2
12.Ng1

p44, Taking the Attacker
1. Example
2. a5xB
3. QxQ
4. NxR
5. Qxc5
6. RxR

p45, Move Away
1. Example
2. Bd5
3. Rh2
4. Bh7
5. Qxd4
6. e4e3

p46, Protect
1. Example
2. Nb4
3. Rd2
4. Kf8
5. Kc4
6. b7b6

p47, Block
1. d7d6
2. Bc5
3. Example
4. Nf3
5. Rf2 or Bf2
6. Ng7

p48, Find 2 Ways
1. Ne2 or c2c3
2. Kb3 or c4c5
3. Ne1 or Kc2
4. Rg1 or Qd7
5. Guide
6. Nf5 or f7f6 (or f7f5)
7. d3d4 or Ng7
8. Qf7 or Qh2
9. h2h4 or d2d3
10.Nh6 or Bh5
11.Be5 or Bd8
12.Ne2 or Bxc5

p50, Get out of Check
1. Example
2. Kc8
3. Kd8
4. Ka7
5. Guide
6. RxR
7. QxB
8. NxN
9. a4xB
10.Rg7
11.Be2
12.Kd1

p52, Castling
1. No
2. No
3. No
4. Yes
5. No
6. No

p53, Defending /Mix
1. e2e3
2. Bg3
3. Re8
4. Qd2
5. c5c6
6. Qxd5
7. Ba5
8. Bd2
9. Bb5
10. Rd5 or Re4
11.Nd6
12.KxN

p56, Checkmate with a Rook
1. Example
2. Rc8#
3. Rh3#
4. Rh2#
5. Rb8#
6. Ra6#
7. Rc1#
8. Rc8#
9. Rg8#

p57, Checkmate with a Bishop
1. Bb2#
2. Bd4#
3. Bc6#
4. Bc2#
5. Bd5#
6. Bf5#
7. Bd7#
8. Bf6#
9. Bh4#

**p58, Checkmate
with a Knight**
1. Nc3#
2. Ng6#
3. Ng3#
4. Nf3#
5. Ng6#
6. Nd3#
7. Nc2#
8. Nxf7#
9. Nf6#

**p59, Checkmate
with a Pawn**
10.b3b2#
11.b7b8=Q# (or R)
12.d3d2#
13.e2e1=Q# (or R)
14.a7a8=Q# (or R)
15.f6xg5#
16.c2c1=Q#
17.a4xb5# or c4xb5#
18.b7b8=N#

**p60, Checkmate
with a Queen**
1. Qg2#
2. Qa4#
3. Qc1#
4. Qg3#
5. Qg8#
6. Qg3#
7. Qh1#
8. Qc7#
9. Qd7#

**p62, Checkmate
in 1 move / A**
1. Qg7#
2. Qb4#
3. Qh3#

4. Ra2#
5. Qb7#
6. Ra6#

**p63, Checkmate
in 1 move / B**
1. Ra7#
2. Rb1#
3. Bf1#
4. Nc3#
5. Ne6#
6. g7g5#

p64, Creating Checkmate
1. Qg4#
2. Qc7#
3. Qb2#
4. Qg7#
5. Qg1#
6. Qb7#

**p66, Creating
Checkmate / B**
1. Rh1#
2. Qb7# or Qa8#
3. Bc4#
4. Nh6#
5. Re8#
6. Nf2#

**p67, Creating
Checkmate / C**
1. Bc3#
2. Re3#
3. Qc8#
4. Qf8#
5. Bh7#
6. Be1# or Bf2#

**p71, Favourable
Exchange**
1. Example
2. f5xR Bxe6
3. NxR KxN
4. BxR RxB
5. NxR e6xN
6. g5xN e3xf4
7. RxQ BxR
8. BxR RxB
9. NxR BxN
10.d4xN b2xc3
11.BxQ g3xB
12.RxQ KxR

p74, Mix
1. Bd4
2. Kg7
3. Bg3 or Bf4
4. Nxd4
5. Rxd2
6. Qxa5

**p78, Chess Ladder
Final Test A**
1. Rc3+
2. Bxc7+
3. Rd4
4. BxN
5. Nb7#
6. Bf5#

**p79, Chess Ladder
Final Test B**
1. BxR NxB
2. BxR+ KxB
3. c4c3#
4. Nh3#
5. Ng4+ or NxB+
6. Qe5+

Credits

This book would not be what it is without the generous media support offered by the following entities and individuals:

Picture of Xiangqi, p6: Inductiveload, Public domain, via Wikimedia Commons

Picture of Wilhelm Steinitz, p7: https://nl.wikipedia.org/wiki/User:Jaapvanderkooij

Picture of Vera Menchik, p7: Unknown photographer (Underwood & Underwood), Public domain, via Wikimedia Commons

Picture of Magnus Carlsen, p7: Andreas Kontokanis from Piraeus, Greece, CC BY-SA 2.0 <https://creativecommons.org/licenses/by-sa/2.0>, via Wikimedia Commons

Picture of Garri Kasparov, p7: Copyright 2007, S.M.S.I., Inc. - Owen Williams, The Kasparov Agency., CC BY-SA 3.0 <http://creativecommons.org/licenses/by-sa/3.0/>, via Wikimedia Commons